DIRTY MONEY

THE ANATOMY OF CORRUPTION

DIPAN KUMAR DAS

SUDIP KUMAR DAS

This work is dedicated to all those who tirelessly strive for a world marked by integrity, transparency, and ethical conduct. To the whistleblowers who risk their safety to expose corruption, the advocates for change who tirelessly work to create a better future, and the leaders who champion ethical practices in their organizations and communities, your commitment inspires us.

May this dedication serve as a reminder of the importance of your efforts and the shared vision of a world where corruption's shadows recede, and the light of integrity and transparency prevails. Your dedication is the beacon of hope that guides us towards a more just and equitable world.

Foreword

In the world's grand narrative, corruption has long held a prominent and notorious role. It has played a part in shaping the destinies of nations, the fates of individuals, and the landscapes of both public and private institutions. Yet, despite its pervasive presence, corruption remains a subject of persistent inquiry and debate, as societies grapple with its causes, consequences, and the means to combat it.

This exploration into the labyrinth of corruption invites readers to embark on a profound journey. It is a journey that navigates the clandestine corridors of power, the ethical dilemmas faced by individuals, and the transformative potential of collective action. Through these pages, we venture into the historical roots of corruption, the intricate ways it manifests in government and corporate structures, and the vital role of whistle-blowers in unmasking its hidden facets.

Corruption's impacts reverberate across the globe, undermining social cohesion, eroding trust in institutions, and perpetuating cycles of poverty and inequality. In every corner of the world, there are those who continue to experience its human toll. This exploration offers an opportunity to understand the profound costs of corruption and to reflect upon the collective imperative to alleviate them.

Yet, this journey is not one of despair, for it is illuminated by the hope that genuine change is possible. The stories of progress and the collective efforts to combat corruption remind us that the battle against corruption is not in vain. As we delve into the complexities of this topic, we encounter the power of transparency, accountability, and ethical leadership to reshape the contours of society.

The fight against corruption demands our unceasing commitment, and this exploration is both an invitation and a guide on this collective endeavor. By uniting individuals, organizations, and governments in a shared commitment to integrity, transparency, and ethical behavior, we can progress toward a world that is more just and fair. It is my sincere hope that this work will inspire and inform those who seek a brighter, more transparent, and ethically grounded future.

May this journey serve as a testament to the human spirit's enduring resilience, the power of collaboration, and the unwavering pursuit of a world free from the shackles of corruption.

Preface

In the interconnected tapestry of our global society, the issue of corruption stands as a persistent and challenging thread. It weaves through the fabric of nations, governments, and institutions, affecting the lives of countless individuals. This exploration into the intricate phenomenon of corruption seeks to untangle the complexities that shroud it and shed light on the pathways to transparency and integrity.

Corruption knows no bounds, manifesting in various forms, from the subtle misuse of power to the grand scale of embezzlement and fraud. Its far-reaching consequences touch economies, societies, and the lives of people who must endure its burdens. The individuals who dare to expose its hidden face play a pivotal role in our collective journey toward accountability and ethics.

In this exploration, we embark on a multidimensional voyage through history, psychology, and the real-world examples of corruption. We examine the global impact of corruption and its role in government, corporate, and law enforcement sectors. We seek to understand how the potent forces of power and greed can lead individuals and organizations astray, sometimes with devastating consequences.

As we traverse this complex landscape, we encounter high-profile corruption cases and scandals from various corners of the globe. These case studies serve as stark reminders of the insidious nature of corruption and the importance of vigilance and ethical conduct.

The chapters contained within these pages invite readers to reflect on the challenges that persist in the battle against corruption. We delve into the significance of transparency, accountability, and ethical leadership, recognizing their potential to pave the way for a world marked by integrity. Along the way, we acknowledge the hurdles and complexities that confront those who strive for a more just and transparent society.

Ultimately, this exploration is a call to action. It is a call to individuals, organizations, and governments to play their part in creating a world that values ethics, integrity, and transparency. It is an invitation to join the collective endeavor to address corruption's roots and foster a brighter, more equitable future.

As we set forth on this journey through the intricate terrain of corruption, may we find inspiration, insight, and a renewed commitment to the pursuit of a world where ethics and integrity triumph over secrecy and deceit.

Prologue

In the grand theater of human history, there exists a recurring character, one that plays a role both behind the scenes and in the spotlight, shaping the destinies of nations and individuals alike. This character is corruption, a formidable adversary that transcends borders and boundaries, infiltrating governments, corporations, and the daily lives of people.

Our exploration into the depths of this enigmatic phenomenon is a journey into the shadows, where ethical boundaries blur and moral compasses waver. As we embark on this exploration, we find ourselves tracing the origins of corruption, dissecting its various forms, and unveiling the intricate ways it insinuates itself into the fabric of society.

Throughout this narrative, we will encounter the psychological and sociological factors that underpin corruption, examining the complex interplay of power, greed, and moral compromise. We will scrutinize high-profile cases, where individuals and entities have been seduced by the allure of illicit gains, often with profound consequences.

Yet, amid the darkness, we will also find sparks of light. Stories of individuals who defy the status quo, who risk everything to expose corruption's hidden truths. We will witness the transformative power of transparency and ethical leadership, and we will celebrate the resilience of societies that have cast off the chains of corruption.

This exploration is an invitation to delve into the complexities of an issue that affects us all. It is a call to action, a reminder that the battle against corruption is a collective endeavor, one that demands our vigilance, our commitment to ethics, and our unwavering pursuit of a world marked by transparency and integrity.

As we embark on this journey through the intricate terrain of corruption, may we find enlightenment, inspiration, and the shared resolve to illuminate the path to a more just and equitable future.

CHAPTER ONE
Introduction to Corruption

Defining Corruption and Its Various Forms

In the shadows of every society, corruption lurks like a persistent specter, undermining the very foundations of trust, integrity, and justice. It is a phenomenon that transcends geographical boundaries, cultural norms, and political ideologies, casting its dark shadow on both developed and developing nations alike. To understand the intricacies of this pervasive issue, we must first embark on a journey to define corruption and explore its multifaceted forms.

1.1 What is Corruption?

Corruption is a complex and elusive concept that has been subject to numerous interpretations over the years. At its core, corruption involves the abuse of power, position, or authority for personal gain or the benefit of a select few. It represents a deviation from the principles of honesty, transparency, and ethical conduct that society expects from its institutions and individuals.

1.2 The Various Forms of Corruption

Corruption manifests itself in a myriad of ways, often blurring the lines between legality and illegality. Here are some of the most prevalent forms:

1.2.1 Bribery

Bribery involves the offering, giving, receiving, or soliciting of something of value (usually money) to influence the actions of an official or other person in a position of authority. It can occur in both the public and private sectors and is a common entry point for corrupt practices.

1.2.2 Embezzlement

Embezzlement occurs when a person entrusted with the funds or property of others misappropriates those assets for personal use. This often takes place within organizations, where employees or executives divert funds for personal gain.

1.2.3 Extortion

Extortion is the act of obtaining something (money, property, services, etc.) through coercion or threats. Corrupt individuals may use intimidation or violence to force others into compliance, leading to a cycle of corruption and fear.

1.2.4 Nepotism and Cronyism

Nepotism involves favoring family members or close friends in matters of hiring, promotion, or resource allocation, regardless of their qualifications. Cronyism is a similar practice that extends to a broader network of personal connections.

1.2.5 Patronage

Patronage refers to the distribution of positions, contracts, or favors by those in power to their supporters or allies. It often leads to the appointment of unqualified individuals to important positions.

1.2.6 Money Laundering

Money laundering is the process of making illegally obtained money appear legitimate by passing it through a complex sequence of banking transfers or commercial transactions. It plays a crucial role in obscuring the origins of "dirty money."

1.3 The Widespread Impact of Corruption

Corruption is not a victimless crime. Its effects are far-reaching and can be felt across society, affecting individuals, businesses, and governments. Some of the consequences of corruption include:

Erosion of public trust in institutions

Diversion of resources away from essential services

Undermining of fair competition in business

Reinforcement of inequality and social injustice

Stifling of economic growth and development

In the chapters that follow, we will delve deeper into the roots of corruption, its historical context, and its contemporary manifestations. We will also explore the efforts and strategies aimed at combating corruption, as well as the ongoing challenges in the quest for a more transparent and ethical world. As we journey through the intricate web of corruption, we will strive to unravel its complexities and shed light on the path towards a corruption-free society.

Historical Context and Evolution of Corruption

To comprehend the full scope of corruption, we must trace its historical roots and examine how it has evolved over time. Corruption is not a recent phenomenon; it has deep historical ties and has adapted to changing societal, political, and economic contexts.

2.1 Ancient Origins

Corruption has ancient origins, with records of corrupt practices dating back thousands of years. In the early city-states of Mesopotamia, for example, there were instances of bribery and embezzlement. Similarly, ancient Rome saw the rise of corrupt officials who exploited their positions for personal gain. These historical examples underscore that corruption is an enduring aspect of human behavior.

2.2 Feudalism and Patronage Systems

During the feudal era in Europe, the relationship between lords and vassals often involved practices resembling corruption. Lords would grant land and protection to vassals in exchange for loyalty and military service, but this system was prone to abuse as lords could exploit their power. Patronage networks, in which rulers appointed loyal supporters to positions of authority, also contributed to corruption in many societies.

2.3 Colonialism and Corruption

Colonialism had a profound impact on the evolution of corruption, particularly in regions colonized by European powers. Colonial administrators often engaged in corrupt practices, exploiting the resources of colonized nations for their own gain. This legacy of corruption in some former colonies continues to affect these nations today.

2.4 Modernization and Bureaucracy

The advent of modern nation-states and bureaucratic systems brought new opportunities for corruption. As governments expanded and bureaucracies grew, corruption found fertile ground in the complex web of regulations, licenses, and permits. Public officials could demand bribes to expedite or facilitate various processes.

2.5 The Cold War and Geopolitical Corruption

The Cold War era witnessed corruption on a global scale, with superpowers like the United States and the Soviet Union supporting corrupt regimes in pursuit of geopolitical interests. This period saw the entrenchment of corrupt leaders in various countries, with far-reaching consequences for their citizens.

2.6 Transparency Movements

The late 20th and early 21st centuries witnessed a growing global awareness of the detrimental effects of corruption. Transparency and anti-corruption movements gained momentum, leading to international agreements and organizations dedicated to combating corruption. The United Nations Convention against Corruption (UNCAC) is a notable example of such efforts.

2.7 Digital Age and New Frontiers of Corruption

The digital age has introduced new forms of corruption, such as cybercrime, online fraud, and the misuse of technology for corrupt practices. These challenges demonstrate the adaptability of corruption in the face of technological advancements.

2.8 Cultural and Societal Factors

It is essential to acknowledge that the perception and acceptance of corruption can vary across cultures and societies. What one culture may consider a norm, another may view as corruption. Understanding these cultural nuances is crucial when addressing corruption in a global context.

2.9 Conclusion

The historical journey of corruption reveals its persistence and adaptability throughout human history. It has evolved alongside changes in governance, economics, and technology, making it a formidable challenge to address. As we move forward in our exploration of corruption, it is imperative to consider its historical context to gain a deeper understanding of its roots and manifestations in contemporary society. In the following chapters, we will delve into specific aspects of corruption, its impact on various sectors, and the ongoing efforts to combat this deeply ingrained issue.

The Global Impact of Corruption on Society

Corruption is not merely a local or regional issue; its consequences ripple across borders and societies, affecting individuals, communities, and nations on a global scale. In this chapter, we will explore the profound impact of corruption and how it undermines the social fabric, hampers economic progress, and jeopardizes the well-being of people around the world.

3.1 Undermining Trust and Confidence

One of the most immediate and pervasive effects of corruption is the erosion of public trust and confidence in institutions. When people believe that their government, businesses, or institutions are corrupt, they become disillusioned and cynical. This lack of trust can lead to social unrest, political instability, and a breakdown of social cohesion.

3.2 Economic Consequences

Corruption has a crippling impact on economic development. It diverts resources away from productive investments and essential public services, such as education, healthcare, and infrastructure. The following are key economic repercussions:

Reduced Foreign Direct Investment (FDI): Corruption discourages foreign investors, as it introduces uncertainty and increases business costs.

Inefficient Allocation of Resources: Resources are allocated based on bribery and favoritism rather than merit, leading to economic inefficiency.

Wealth Inequality: Corruption often exacerbates wealth inequality as a select few accumulate wealth through corrupt practices, while the majority struggle in poverty.

Stifled Innovation: A corrupt environment discourages innovation, as individuals and businesses are less likely to invest in research and development in a climate of uncertainty.

3.3 Social Injustice and Inequality

Corruption perpetuates social injustice and inequality by favoring a select few at the expense of the many. When individuals can buy advantages and escape consequences through bribery, those without financial means are left at a significant disadvantage. This exacerbates existing social disparities and prevents equitable access to opportunities and resources.

3.4 Health and Education

Corruption can have dire consequences for healthcare and

education. Funds meant for hospitals and schools may be siphoned off, leaving facilities ill-equipped and understaffed. This impacts the quality of services and can lead to preventable deaths and reduced educational outcomes, perpetuating a cycle of poverty and limited upward mobility.

3.5 Security and Stability

Insecurity and instability often accompany corruption. When law enforcement and security agencies are compromised, crime rates can soar, and organized crime can flourish. This has global security implications, as regions with high levels of corruption may become hotspots for conflict and terrorism.

3.6 Environmental Degradation

Corruption can also contribute to environmental degradation. Illegally logging forests, allowing polluters to evade regulations, and engaging in corrupt practices in the extraction industries can lead to deforestation, pollution, and habitat destruction, with far-reaching ecological consequences.

3.7 Global Trade and Investment

Corruption can distort global trade and investment patterns. When bribes and kickbacks influence trade decisions, it disrupts fair competition and can harm businesses in both developed and developing nations. It also creates barriers to international development by stifling investment in countries with high corruption levels.

3.8 Human Rights Abuses

In regions where corruption is rampant, human rights abuses often go unchecked. Corrupt officials may engage in extrajudicial killings, arbitrary detention, and other forms of abuse without facing consequences. This threatens the fundamental rights and dignity of individuals.

3.9 International Relations and Diplomacy

Corruption can strain international relations and diplomacy. Countries may use corruption allegations as a tool for political leverage, leading to tensions and strained relationships between nations.

3.10 Conclusion

The global impact of corruption is vast and multifaceted, affecting nearly every aspect of society and governance. Understanding the far-reaching consequences of corruption is essential in motivating individuals, organizations, and governments to take action against this pervasive issue. In subsequent chapters, we will explore efforts to combat corruption, both on a national and international level, and examine case studies that illustrate the real-world impact of corruption on societies around the globe.

CHAPTER TWO

The Roots of Corruption

Exploring the Psychological and Sociological Factors that Contribute to Corruption

Corruption is a deeply ingrained societal problem that cannot be fully understood without considering the underlying psychological and sociological factors that drive individuals and institutions toward unethical behavior. In this chapter, we delve into the human aspects of corruption, examining the psychological and sociological factors that contribute to its emergence and persistence.

2.1 The Psychological Factors

2.1.1 Greed and Self-Interest

Greed and the pursuit of personal gain are fundamental psychological drivers of corruption. Individuals may engage in corrupt practices when they prioritize their own financial or personal interests over ethical considerations.

2.1.2 Moral Disengagement

People often use cognitive mechanisms to justify their unethical actions. Moral disengagement is a process where individuals distance themselves from the moral consequences of their behavior. This can involve minimizing the harm caused by corruption or blaming external factors.

2.1.3 Rationalization

Corrupt individuals may rationalize their actions by convincing themselves that their behavior is justifiable. They might argue that everyone else is doing it, that they deserve the benefits, or that they are merely playing by the rules of a corrupt system.

2.1.4 Social Identity and Conformity

People's sense of identity and belonging to certain groups can influence their behavior. When corruption is prevalent within a group or organization, individuals may conform to the group's norms and engage in corrupt practices to fit in.

2.1.5 Lack of Empathy

A lack of empathy toward potential victims of corruption can make it easier for individuals to engage in unethical behavior. They may not fully consider the harm their actions cause to others.

2.2 The Sociological Factors

2.2.1 Institutional Corruption

Institutions and organizations can create environments that foster corruption. When corrupt practices are systemic and go unpunished, individuals within those institutions may feel compelled to engage in corrupt behavior to advance their careers or protect their positions.

2.2.2 Weak Rule of Law

Societies with weak rule of law, where laws are not consistently enforced or where legal systems are easily manipulated, are more susceptible to corruption. In such environments, individuals may believe they can act with impunity.

2.2.3 Cultural Norms

Cultural norms and societal attitudes toward corruption play a significant role in shaping behavior. In some cultures, corruption may be more tolerated or even seen as a means of survival or social mobility.

2.2.4 Economic Inequality

High levels of economic inequality can create a breeding ground for corruption. When a small elite controls significant wealth and resources, those who lack access to opportunities may resort to corruption as a means of leveling the playing field.

2.2.5 Lack of Accountability

The absence of effective mechanisms for holding individuals and institutions accountable for corrupt acts can embolden corrupt behavior. When there is little risk of punishment, people may be more likely to engage in corruption.

2.3 Conclusion

Understanding the psychological and sociological factors that contribute to corruption is essential for developing effective strategies to combat it. These factors interact in complex ways, and addressing corruption requires a multifaceted approach that considers both the individual motivations and the societal conditions that enable corrupt practices. In the following chapters, we will examine specific manifestations of corruption in government, business, and other sectors, and explore the strategies and efforts aimed at mitigating its impact.

How Power and Greed Can Lead Individuals and Organizations Astray

Power and greed are potent forces that, when unchecked, can drive individuals and organizations to engage in unethical and corrupt behavior. In this chapter, we explore how these human motivations can influence decision-making and lead down the path of corruption.

2.1 The Corrupting Influence of Power

2.1.1 Power as a Magnet for Corruption

Power, whether political, economic, or social, can be a magnet for corruption. The allure of power often leads individuals to seek and consolidate power at any cost, including through unethical means.

2.1.2 Hubris and Entitlement

Those in positions of power may develop a sense of hubris and entitlement, believing that the rules don't apply to them. This can lead to a disregard for ethical constraints and a willingness to engage in corrupt practices.

2.1.3 Lack of Accountability

Powerful individuals and organizations often face less scrutiny and accountability for their actions. This perceived immunity can embolden them to engage in corrupt behavior, believing they will not be held responsible.

2.1.4 Patronage and Nepotism

Powerful individuals may use their positions to benefit friends, family, or loyal supporters through patronage and nepotism, even if it means compromising ethical standards.

2.2 The Greed Factor

2.2.1 The Pursuit of Wealth

Greed, the insatiable desire for wealth and material possessions, can cloud judgment and lead individuals and organizations to prioritize financial gain over ethical considerations.

2.2.2 Short-Term Gain vs. Long-Term Consequences

Greed often drives individuals and organizations to prioritize short-term financial gains over long-term sustainability and ethical principles. This can result in risky and unsustainable practices.

2.2.3 Competition and Rivalry

In competitive environments, the desire to outperform rivals and achieve financial success can lead to unethical behaviors such as bribery, price-fixing, and fraud.

2.2.4 Psychological Traps

Greed can trap individuals in a cycle of continuously seeking more wealth, even when they already possess substantial resources. This can lead to unethical and criminal behavior to maintain or increase wealth.

2.3 The Intersection of Power and Greed

2.3.1 The Perfect Storm

When power and greed intersect, individuals and organizations may find themselves in a perfect storm of corruption. The unchecked pursuit of both power and wealth can lead to egregious acts of corruption and abuse.

2.3.2 Corporate Corruption

In the corporate world, the pursuit of profit and market dominance can drive organizations to engage in corrupt practices such as insider trading, accounting fraud, and anticompetitive behavior.

2.3.3 Political Corruption

In politics, the quest for power can lead to political corruption, including vote-buying, embezzlement, and cronyism, all of which undermine democratic processes.

2.4 The Role of Oversight and Accountability

2.4.1 Mitigating Power and Greed

Effective oversight mechanisms, transparency, and accountability measures are essential for mitigating the corrupting influence of power and greed. These mechanisms can help deter unethical behavior and hold wrongdoers accountable.

2.4.2 Ethics Education

Promoting ethics education and awareness within organizations and society can help individuals recognize and resist the corrupting influences of power and greed.

2.5 Conclusion

Power and greed are powerful motivators that can lead individuals and organizations astray, fostering corruption and unethical behavior. Recognizing the role of these motivations is crucial for implementing effective anti-corruption measures and promoting ethical conduct. In the subsequent chapters, we will examine real-world examples of corruption in various sectors and explore strategies for preventing and combatting corruption in the face of these powerful influences.

here are some case studies of infamous corrupt individuals and entities from various parts of the world:

Enron Corporation (USA):

Enron, once one of the largest energy companies in the world, collapsed in 2001 due to massive accounting fraud. Top executives engaged in financial manipulation, concealing debts, and inflating profits to deceive investors and regulators. This scandal resulted in job losses and wiped out billions of dollars in shareholder value.

Bernie Madoff (USA):

Bernie Madoff operated one of the most significant Ponzi schemes in history. Over several decades, he defrauded investors of billions of dollars by promising high returns while using new investments to pay earlier investors. The scheme collapsed in 2008, leading to Madoff's arrest and a 150-year prison sentence.

Viktor Yanukovych (Ukraine):

Viktor Yanukovych, Ukraine's former president, faced allegations of widespread corruption during his presidency. The "Euromaidan" protests in 2014 were sparked by his government's corruption and led to his ousting. Investigations revealed extravagant lifestyles and embezzlement of state funds.

Lula da Silva (Brazil):

Luiz Inácio Lula da Silva, former president of Brazil, faced corruption charges related to the Operation Car Wash scandal. He was accused of accepting bribes and kickbacks from construction companies in exchange for government contracts. While his supporters argued the charges were politically motivated, he was convicted and briefly imprisoned.

FIFA (International):

The Fédération Internationale de Football Association (FIFA) faced allegations of corruption involving top officials. This scandal included accusations of bribery in the selection of World Cup host countries and led to numerous arrests and resignations within the organization.

Najib Razak (Malaysia):

Malaysia's former Prime Minister, Najib Razak, was embroiled in a massive financial scandal known as the 1MDB scandal. He was accused of embezzling billions of dollars from a state investment fund and using the money for personal expenses, including luxury real estate and artwork.

Silvio Berlusconi (Italy):

Silvio Berlusconi, the former Prime Minister of Italy, faced numerous legal battles and allegations of corruption during his political career.

These included charges related to tax fraud, bribery, and alleged links to organized crime.

Jiang Zemin's Family (China):

Allegations of corruption have swirled around the family of former Chinese President Jiang Zemin. Family members were accused of amassing wealth through corrupt practices and connections, raising questions about the extent of corruption within China's political elite.

Jacob Zuma (South Africa):

Jacob Zuma, the former President of South Africa, faced numerous corruption allegations during his tenure. The most prominent case involved allegations of a corrupt relationship with the Gupta family, leading to his resignation in 2018.

Yulia Tymoshenko (Ukraine):

Yulia Tymoshenko, a former Prime Minister of Ukraine, faced corruption charges related to a controversial gas deal with Russia. Critics argued that the charges were politically motivated, but she was convicted and later released.

Yanukovych Family (Ukraine):

Alongside former President Viktor Yanukovych, his family members, including his son Oleksandr, faced allegations of corruption. They were accused of accumulating vast wealth through embezzlement and corrupt practices while in power.

Ferdinand Marcos (Philippines):

Ferdinand Marcos, the former President of the Philippines, and his wife, Imelda, were accused of embezzling billions of dollars from the country's coffers during their lengthy rule. Imelda Marcos famously amassed a vast shoe collection, symbolizing the excesses of their regime.

Slobodan Milosevic (Yugoslavia/Serbia):

Slobodan Milosevic, the former President of Yugoslavia and later Serbia, faced allegations of corruption and embezzlement during his rule. His leadership was marked by economic mismanagement and allegations of funds siphoned off for personal gain.

Yoshiro Mori (Japan):

Yoshiro Mori, a former Prime Minister of Japan, faced allegations of financial impropriety during his time in office. He was accused of accepting illicit donations from a scandal-plagued company and subsequently resigned from his position.

Rafael Correa (Ecuador):

Rafael Correa, former President of Ecuador, was accused of corruption related to public contracts and misappropriation of funds during his presidency. His administration faced allegations of suppressing dissent and manipulating the judiciary.

Zhang Shuguang (China):

Zhang Shuguang, a high-ranking official in China's National Energy Administration, was involved in one of China's most significant corruption cases. He was found guilty of embezzling millions of dollars in bribes and kickbacks related to energy contracts.

Siemens AG (Germany):

Siemens AG, one of Germany's largest conglomerates, faced a massive bribery scandal in the mid-2000s. The company was accused of engaging in a systematic practice of paying bribes to win contracts worldwide, resulting in hefty fines and reputational damage.

Alberto Fujimori (Peru):

Alberto Fujimori, the former President of Peru, was convicted of embezzlement, bribery, and human rights abuses during his presidency. He fled to Japan to avoid prosecution but was later extradited and imprisoned.

Kim Jong-un (North Korea):

Kim Jong-un, the Supreme Leader of North Korea, has faced allegations of corruption, including embezzlement of state funds and engaging in illicit activities to maintain his regime's power.

Petrobras (Brazil):

Brazil's state-owned oil company, Petrobras, was embroiled in one of the largest corruption scandals in Latin American history. High-level executives and politicians were implicated in a massive kickback scheme involving billions of dollars.

2G Spectrum Scandal:

The 2G spectrum scandal involved the misallocation of 2G (second-generation) mobile spectrum licenses by the government in 2008. It led to allegations of underpricing and corruption in the allocation process, resulting in significant financial losses to the Indian exchequer. Several high-profile politicians, including A. Raja and Kanimozhi, faced charges in this case.

Commonwealth Games Scam:

The 2010 Commonwealth Games in Delhi were marred by allegations of corruption and mismanagement. It was revealed that significant funds were siphoned off through inflated contracts and irregularities in awarding contracts for the construction of sports facilities and infrastructure.

Coal Allocation Scam:

The coal allocation scam involved irregularities in the allocation of coal blocks to private companies by the government. It was alleged that the allocations were made without a transparent bidding process, leading to financial losses. This scandal implicated several politicians and business leaders.

Adarsh Housing Society Scam:

The Adarsh Housing Society scam centered around a housing project in Mumbai meant for war veterans and widows. It was alleged that influential politicians, bureaucrats, and military officials secured flats in the society by manipulating eligibility criteria and clearances.

Satyam Computer Services Scandal:

Satyam Computer Services, one of India's largest IT companies, faced a massive corporate fraud scandal in 2009. The company's founder and chairman, Ramalinga Raju, admitted to inflating the company's financial figures to the tune of billions of dollars, shaking confidence in India's corporate governance.

Bofors Scandal:

The Bofors scandal, which came to light in the late 1980s, involved allegations of kickbacks in a defense deal between India and the Swedish arms manufacturer AB Bofors. The scandal had political repercussions and led to the downfall of the government at the time.

Vyapam Scam:

The Vyapam (Vyavsayik Pariksha Mandal) scam was a massive admission and recruitment scandal in the Indian state of Madhya Pradesh. It involved irregularities in the conduct of entrance exams for professional courses and government job recruitments. Many individuals, including politicians and government officials, were implicated.

Saradha Group Chit Fund Scam:

The Saradha Group chit fund scam was a financial fraud that affected several states in India, primarily West Bengal. The group collected deposits from investors promising high returns but ultimately defaulted, resulting in significant losses for investors. Prominent politicians and leaders of the Saradha Group faced charges in this case.

CHAPTER THREE

Corruption in Government

Analyzing Corruption within Government Institutions

Corruption within government institutions is a pervasive problem that undermines trust in public administration, erodes the rule of law, and hampers societal progress. In this chapter, we delve into the various facets of corruption within government, examining its causes, manifestations, and consequences.

3.1 The Nature of Corruption in Government

3.1.1 Bureaucratic Corruption

Bureaucratic corruption refers to corrupt practices within government agencies and institutions. This can include bribery, embezzlement, nepotism, and favoritism in public procurement, licensing, and regulatory processes.

3.1.2 Political Corruption

Political corruption involves politicians and elected officials abusing their positions for personal gain or to advance their political interests. This can include accepting bribes, engaging in vote-buying, and manipulating elections.

3.1.3 Police and Law Enforcement Corruption

Corruption within law enforcement agencies can take the form of bribery, extortion, abuse of power, and the manipulation of evidence. It can undermine public safety and justice.

3.1.4 Judicial Corruption

Judicial corruption undermines the integrity of the judiciary, affecting the fairness and impartiality of legal proceedings. This can include bribery, influence-peddling, and political interference in the judiciary.

3.2 Causes of Corruption in Government

3.2.1 Lack of Transparency

A lack of transparency in government operations can create opportunities for corruption to thrive. When government actions and decisions are shielded from public scrutiny, corrupt practices can go undetected.

3.2.2 Weak Rule of Law

A weak rule of law, where legal enforcement is inconsistent or easily manipulated, can encourage corrupt behavior within government institutions.

3.2.3 Political Patronage

The practice of political patronage, where government positions and benefits are awarded to supporters and allies, can foster corruption as officials prioritize loyalty over merit.

3.2.4 Low Salaries and Inadequate Oversight

Low salaries for government officials, coupled with inadequate oversight and enforcement mechanisms, can make corruption more tempting as a means of supplementing income.

3.3 Manifestations of Government Corruption

3.3.1 Bribery and Kickbacks

Bribery involves the exchange of money, gifts, or favors in return for official actions or decisions. Kickbacks are a form of bribery where a portion of funds is returned to the corrupt official.

3.3.2 Embezzlement

Embezzlement occurs when government officials misappropriate public funds or assets for personal use. This can include diverting public funds into private accounts.

3.3.3 Nepotism and Cronyism

Nepotism and cronyism involve government officials favoring family members, friends, or close associates in hiring, promotions, and the allocation of government resources.

3.3.4 Abuse of Power

Corruption often involves the abuse of power by government officials for personal gain or to suppress dissent and opposition.

3.4 Consequences of Government Corruption

3.4.1 Erosion of Trust

Corruption erodes public trust in government institutions, diminishing citizens' confidence in their leaders' ability to act in the public interest.

3.4.2 Economic Consequences

Government corruption can hinder economic growth, deter foreign investment, and result in the misallocation of resources, leading to economic inefficiency.

3.4.3 Inequality and Injustice

Corruption can exacerbate social inequalities and perpetuate injustice, as it often benefits a select few while harming the broader population.

3.4.4 Political Instability

Corruption can lead to political instability and unrest, as citizens become disillusioned with corrupt governments and seek change through protests and demonstrations.

3.5 Conclusion

Corruption within government institutions is a multifaceted problem with far-reaching consequences. Addressing government corruption requires a comprehensive approach that includes transparency measures, legal reforms, and robust anti-corruption mechanisms. In the following chapters, we will explore strategies for combating government corruption and examine real-world examples of efforts to promote transparency and integrity in government.

Understanding the Dynamics and Implications of Political Corruption

Political corruption is a pervasive and deeply troubling issue that plagues governments worldwide. In this chapter, we delve into the dynamics of political corruption, its various forms, and the far-reaching consequences it has on societies and democracies.

4.1 Forms of Political Corruption

4.1.1 Bribery

Bribery in politics involves the offering, giving, receiving, or soliciting of money, gifts, or favors to influence political decisions, policies, or actions. It can take place at all levels of government and can compromise the integrity of political processes.

4.1.2 Embezzlement

Embezzlement within political circles refers to the misappropriation of public funds or resources by politicians or government officials for personal gain. This often involves diverting state funds or assets into private accounts or projects.

4.1.3 Vote-Buying

Vote-buying occurs when politicians or their agents provide monetary incentives or gifts to voters in exchange for their support during elections. This corrupt practice undermines the democratic process by manipulating the outcome of elections.

4.1.4 Nepotism and Cronyism

Nepotism and cronyism in politics involve the preferential treatment of family members, friends, or associates when making political appointments or awarding government contracts. This can lead to the concentration of power and resources among a select few.

4.1.5 Patronage Networks

Patronage networks in politics are informal systems where politicians grant political favors, appointments, or resources to individuals or groups in exchange for loyalty and support. These networks can perpetuate corruption and entrench political elites.

4.2 Causes of Political Corruption

4.2.1 Lack of Accountability

Political corruption often thrives in environments with weak checks and balances, where politicians and officials can act with impunity due to inadequate oversight and accountability mechanisms.

4.2.2 Poverty and Economic Inequality

High levels of poverty and economic inequality can make individuals more susceptible to bribery or vote-buying, as they may see corruption as a means of improving their economic circumstances.

4.2.3 Political Culture and Norms

In some societies, a culture of corruption and a tolerance for unethical behavior in politics can become deeply ingrained, making it challenging to combat political corruption.

4.2.4 Lack of Transparency

A lack of transparency in campaign financing, government operations, and decision-making processes can create opportunities for corrupt practices to thrive without public scrutiny.

4.3 Consequences of Political Corruption

4.3.1 Erosion of Public Trust

Political corruption erodes public trust in government institutions, leading citizens to question the integrity of their elected officials and the democratic process itself.

4.3.2 Ineffective Governance

Corruption can hinder effective governance, as resources are misallocated, policies are skewed in favor of corrupt interests, and decision-making processes become distorted.

4.3.3 Economic Consequences

Political corruption can have detrimental economic effects, discouraging foreign investment, distorting competition, and reducing economic growth and development.

4.3.4 Social Injustice

Corruption can exacerbate social inequalities, as resources and benefits often flow to a privileged few while the majority of citizens suffer the consequences of corrupt policies.

4.3.5 Political Instability

Persistent political corruption can lead to political instability, social unrest, and protests, as citizens demand transparency, accountability, and ethical governance.

4.4 Conclusion

Political corruption is a corrosive force that undermines the foundations of democracy and good governance. It has profound consequences on societies, economies, and the overall well-being of citizens. In the chapters that follow, we will explore strategies for combating political corruption, the role of international organizations in addressing this issue, and real-world examples of countries that have taken steps to promote transparency and integrity in politics.

here are some notable corruption scandals that have occurred in different countries around the world:

Watergate Scandal (USA, 1972):

The Watergate scandal involved the break-in at the Democratic National Committee headquarters by members of President Richard Nixon's administration. It led to a cover-up and obstruction of justice, ultimately resulting in Nixon's resignation in 1974.

Tangentopoli (Italy, 1990s):

Tangentopoli, or "Bribesville," was a series of corruption scandals that rocked Italy in the 1990s. It exposed widespread corruption among politicians, business leaders, and the government, leading to the collapse of the traditional political order.

Adarsh Housing Society Scam (India, 2010):

The Adarsh Housing Society scam involved influential individuals, including politicians and military officers, securing flats in a Mumbai housing society meant for war veterans and widows through manipulation of eligibility criteria and clearances.

Operation Car Wash (Brazil, ongoing):

Operation Car Wash is a massive corruption investigation in Brazil that uncovered a network of corruption involving state-owned oil company Petrobras, politicians, and business leaders. It has led to numerous arrests and convictions.

The Panama Papers (Various Countries, 2016):

The Panama Papers leak revealed the involvement of politicians, celebrities, and business figures from around the world in offshore tax evasion and money laundering schemes facilitated by the Panamanian law firm Mossack Fonseca.

1MDB Scandal (Malaysia, ongoing):

The 1Malaysia Development Berhad (1MDB) scandal involves allegations of embezzlement and corruption linked to former Malaysian Prime Minister Najib Razak and his associates. It is one of the largest financial scandals in Malaysian history.

Lava Jato (Peru, ongoing):

Lava Jato, similar to Brazil's Operation Car Wash, is a major corruption investigation in Peru. It has implicated numerous high-ranking politicians and business leaders in a web of bribery and kickbacks.

Guo Wengui (China, ongoing):

Guo Wengui, a Chinese billionaire living in exile, has made allegations of high-level corruption within the Chinese Communist Party. His claims have exposed internal party strife and corruption allegations involving top officials.

Malabu Oil Scandal (Nigeria, ongoing):

The Malabu Oil scandal revolves around the allocation of lucrative oil blocks in Nigeria and alleged corruption involving government officials and multinational oil companies.

Petrogate (Ecuador, 2020):

Petrogate involved allegations of corruption within the state-owned oil company Petroamazonas in Ecuador. It led to the dismissal of top officials and raised questions about the government's handling of oil revenues.

Snowden Leaks (USA, 2013):

Edward Snowden, a former contractor for the U.S. National Security Agency (NSA), leaked classified documents revealing extensive surveillance programs conducted by the NSA. The leaks raised concerns about government overreach and privacy violations.

Gupta Scandal (South Africa, ongoing):

The Gupta scandal in South Africa involves allegations of state capture by the Gupta family, who are accused of using their close ties to former President Jacob Zuma to influence government decisions and gain access to state resources.

Operation Puerto (Spain, 2006):

Operation Puerto uncovered a widespread blood doping scandal in Spanish cycling and implicated several athletes and doctors in a doping ring that extended beyond cycling into other sports.

SNC-Lavalin Scandal (Canada, ongoing):

The SNC-Lavalin scandal involves allegations of corruption and bribery by Canadian engineering firm SNC-Lavalin in its dealings with the Libyan government. The scandal has raised questions about political interference and corporate ethics in Canada.

FIFA Corruption Scandal (International, 2015):

The FIFA corruption scandal rocked the world of international soccer, with allegations of bribery, kickbacks, and money laundering among high-ranking FIFA officials. The scandal led to several high-profile arrests and reforms within the organization.

Volkswagen Emissions Scandal (Germany, 2015):

The Volkswagen emissions scandal involved the manipulation of emission test results for millions of diesel vehicles worldwide. It led to legal actions, fines, and reputational damage for the automaker.

Anglo Leasing Scandal (Kenya, ongoing):

The Anglo Leasing scandal in Kenya revolves around allegations of corrupt government contracts and the misappropriation of public funds in deals involving security equipment and services.

Nirav Modi PNB Scam (India, 2018):

The Nirav Modi Punjab National Bank (PNB) scam involved fraudulent transactions and letters of undertaking, leading to a massive financial fraud in one of India's largest public sector banks. Nirav Modi, a prominent jeweler, and his associates were accused of orchestrating the scam.

Operation Carne Fraca (Brazil, 2017):

Operation Carne Fraca uncovered corruption and bribery within Brazil's meatpacking industry, with allegations of tainted meat exports and collusion between inspectors and meat companies.

Eroni Kumana Scandal (Solomon Islands, ongoing):

The Eroni Kumana scandal in the Solomon Islands involves allegations of corruption and mismanagement within the country's Ministry of Infrastructure Development. It has raised concerns about the misuse of public funds and government contracts.

These scandals underscore the diverse nature of corruption, affecting countries, industries, and institutions across the globe. They highlight the importance of robust anti-corruption measures, transparency, and accountability in addressing and preventing corruption.

CHAPTER FOUR
Corporate Corruption

Examining Corruption in the Corporate World

Corporate corruption is a persistent global challenge that undermines trust in business, distorts competition, and harms economies and society at large. In this chapter, we explore the multifaceted issue of corporate corruption, its various forms, root causes, and the consequences it carries.

4.1 Forms of Corporate Corruption

4.1.1 Bribery and Kickbacks

Corporate bribery involves offering or accepting bribes, kickbacks, or other illicit payments to secure business advantages, contracts, or favorable treatment. It undermines fair competition and can be illegal under national and international laws.

4.1.2 Accounting Fraud

Accounting fraud within corporations includes the manipulation of financial statements, earnings, or accounting records to misrepresent a company's financial health. This can deceive investors, regulators, and the public.

4.1.3 Insider Trading

Insider trading is the illegal buying or selling of a company's securities based on non-public, material information. It can result in unfair advantages for those with privileged information and harm investors.

4.1.4 Price Fixing and Cartels

Price fixing and cartel activities involve colluding with competitors to manipulate prices, divide markets, or rig bids, often leading to artificially inflated prices and anti-competitive behavior.

4.1.5 Money Laundering

Money laundering is the process of concealing the origins of illicitly obtained funds through a series of transactions. Corporations may unwittingly or intentionally be involved in money laundering activities.

4.2 Causes of Corporate Corruption

4.2.1 Pressure to Achieve Financial Targets

Corporate executives and employees may face immense pressure to meet financial targets, leading some to resort to unethical practices to maintain profitability.

4.2.2 Lack of Ethical Leadership

A corporate culture that lacks ethical leadership and accountability can contribute to corruption as employees may emulate unethical behaviors they witness at higher levels.

4.2.3 Weak Regulatory Oversight

Inadequate regulatory oversight can create an environment where corporations feel they can operate with impunity. Weak enforcement mechanisms may also discourage compliance with anti-corruption laws.

4.2.4 Short-Term Focus

Corporations that prioritize short-term gains over long-term sustainability may engage in corrupt practices that yield immediate financial benefits but harm their long-term reputation and viability.

4.3 Consequences of Corporate Corruption

4.3.1 Erosion of Trust

Corporate corruption erodes trust in businesses, affecting relationships with customers, investors, and the public. It can lead to reputational damage and a loss of shareholder value.

4.3.2 Economic Harm

Corporate corruption can distort markets, reduce competition, and hinder economic growth. It may result in inefficiencies, misallocation of resources, and decreased investor confidence.

4.3.3 Legal and Regulatory Consequences

Companies involved in corporate corruption face legal and regulatory consequences, including fines, sanctions, and legal actions that can damage their financial standing and operations.

4.3.4 Impact on Employees

Employees of corrupt corporations may face ethical dilemmas, job insecurity, and reputational harm. Whistleblowers who expose corruption may also suffer retaliation.

4.3.5 Social and Environmental Consequences

Corporate corruption can have broader social and environmental implications, particularly when it leads to unethical practices such as environmental degradation, unsafe products, or human rights abuses.

4.4 Conclusion

Corporate corruption poses a significant threat to businesses, economies, and society. Addressing it requires a commitment to ethical leadership, robust compliance programs, and a culture of integrity within organizations. In the chapters that follow, we will explore strategies for combating corporate corruption, examine case studies of corporate scandals, and consider the role of stakeholders in promoting transparency and accountability in the corporate world.

Understanding and Combating Corruption in Business

Bribery, fraud, and unethical business practices are pervasive issues that can harm organizations, individuals, and society as a whole. In this chapter, we delve into these corrupt practices, explore their various forms, root causes, and the strategies needed to combat them.

5.1 Forms of Bribery, Fraud, and Unethical Business Practices

5.1.1 Bribery

Bribery in business involves offering, giving, receiving, or soliciting something of value, such as money, gifts, or favors, to gain an unfair business advantage or to influence decisions, contracts, or policies.

5.1.2 Accounting Fraud

Accounting fraud encompasses practices like inflating revenues, hiding expenses, and manipulating financial statements to misrepresent a company's financial health, often with the aim of deceiving investors and stakeholders.

5.1.3 Insider Trading

Insider trading in the business world occurs when individuals trade securities based on non-public, material information. This gives them an unfair advantage and can undermine the fairness of financial markets.

5.1.4 Price Fixing and Cartels

Price fixing and cartel activities involve competitors colluding to manipulate prices, allocate markets, or rig bids. These practices harm fair competition, leading to inflated prices and limited consumer choice.

5.1.5 Kickbacks

Kickbacks involve corrupt payments or favors made to individuals who have influence over business decisions, often with the aim of securing business contracts or favorable treatment.

5.2 Causes of Bribery, Fraud, and Unethical Practices

5.2.1 Pressure to Achieve Financial Targets

The pressure to meet financial targets and shareholder expectations can lead individuals and organizations to engage in unethical practices to maintain profitability and financial success.

5.2.2 Lack of Ethical Leadership

A lack of ethical leadership within organizations can set the tone for unethical behavior, as employees may follow the example set by senior executives who prioritize short-term gains over ethical considerations.

5.2.3 Weak Regulatory Oversight

Inadequate regulatory oversight can create an environment where businesses feel they can engage in corrupt practices with minimal risk of detection or enforcement.

5.2.4 Organizational Culture

An organizational culture that places undue emphasis on profits and ignores ethical principles may foster a climate where bribery, fraud, and unethical practices flourish.

5.3 Consequences of Bribery, Fraud, and Unethical Practices

5.3.1 Reputational Damage

Engaging in bribery, fraud, or unethical practices can cause severe reputational damage to organizations, undermining trust with customers, investors, and stakeholders.

5.3.2 Legal and Financial Consequences

Companies involved in such practices face legal and financial repercussions, including fines, penalties, litigation, and damage to their financial standing.

5.3.3 Erosion of Trust

Bribery, fraud, and unethical practices erode trust not only in the offending organization but also in the business community at large, affecting relationships and the overall business environment.

5.3.4 Economic and Social Harm

These practices can have broader economic and social consequences, including market distortions, reduced competition, and negative impacts on employees, consumers, and the economy.

5.4 Conclusion

Bribery, fraud, and unethical business practices are detrimental to organizations, economies, and society. Combating them requires a commitment to ethical leadership, strong corporate governance, and comprehensive compliance programs. In the chapters that follow, we will explore strategies for preventing and addressing these issues, examine real-world examples of corporate scandals, and consider the role of stakeholders in promoting ethical business practices.

High-profile corporate corruption cases have exposed the extent of unethical practices within some of the world's largest and most well-known companies. Here are some notable examples:

Enron Corporation (USA, 2001):

Enron, once one of the world's largest energy companies, filed for bankruptcy in 2001 due to accounting fraud. Executives engaged in deceptive accounting practices to inflate profits and hide debts, resulting in massive financial losses for investors and employees.

WorldCom (USA, 2002):

WorldCom, a telecommunications giant, filed for bankruptcy in 2002 after revealing a $11 billion accounting fraud. The company inflated its earnings by falsely classifying operating expenses as capital expenditures.

Tyco International (USA, 2002):

Top executives at Tyco, a multinational conglomerate, were involved in embezzlement and fraud, including the unauthorized use of company funds for personal expenses. The scandal led to the resignation and imprisonment of CEO Dennis Kozlowski.

Adelphia Communications (USA, 2002):

Adelphia Communications, a major cable television company, faced allegations of corporate looting and accounting fraud. The company's founder and top executives were accused of embezzling billions of dollars.

Satyam Computer Services (India, 2009):

Satyam Computer Services, one of India's largest IT companies, was embroiled in a corporate fraud scandal when its founder and chairman, Ramalinga Raju, admitted to inflating the company's financial figures by billions of dollars.

Siemens AG (Germany, 2008):

Siemens, a multinational conglomerate, faced allegations of engaging in widespread bribery to secure contracts worldwide. The company ultimately settled with various governments, paying substantial fines.

Volkswagen Emissions Scandal (Germany, 2015):

Volkswagen (VW) admitted to manipulating emissions data in millions of its diesel vehicles worldwide to meet environmental standards. The scandal led to massive recalls, legal actions, and substantial financial penalties.

Wells Fargo (USA, 2016):

Wells Fargo, one of the largest U.S. banks, faced a scandal involving the creation of millions of unauthorized customer accounts to meet sales targets. The unethical practices led to significant fines and the resignation of top executives.

1Malaysia Development Berhad (1MDB) (Malaysia, ongoing):

The 1MDB scandal involves allegations of embezzlement and corruption linked to former Malaysian Prime Minister Najib Razak and his associates. It is one of the largest financial scandals in Malaysian history.

Theranos (USA, 2016):

Theranos, a healthcare technology startup, faced allegations of fraud for misleading investors and patients about the capabilities of its blood-testing technology. The company's founder, Elizabeth Holmes, faced criminal charges.

India has seen its share of high-profile corporate corruption cases that have garnered significant attention both nationally and internationally. Here are some notable examples:

Satyam Computer Services Scandal (2009):

The Satyam scandal is one of the most infamous corporate fraud cases in India. The company's founder and chairman, Ramalinga Raju, admitted to inflating the company's financial figures by billions of dollars. The scandal shook the Indian IT industry and led to legal action against Raju and other executives.

2G Spectrum Scandal (2012):

The 2G spectrum scandal involved the misallocation of 2G mobile spectrum licenses by the government in 2008. It led to allegations of underpricing and corruption in the allocation process, resulting in significant financial losses to the Indian exchequer. Several high-profile politicians, including A. Raja and Kanimozhi, faced charges in this case.

Commonwealth Games Scam (2010):

The 2010 Commonwealth Games in Delhi were marred by allegations of corruption and mismanagement. It was revealed that significant funds were siphoned off through inflated contracts and irregularities in awarding contracts for the construction of sports facilities and infrastructure.

Coal Allocation Scam (2014):

The coal allocation scam involved irregularities in the allocation of coal blocks to private companies by the government. It was alleged that the allocations were made without a transparent bidding process, leading to financial losses. This scandal implicated several politicians and business leaders.

Adarsh Housing Society Scam (2010):

The Adarsh Housing Society scam centered around a housing project in Mumbai meant for war veterans and widows. It was alleged that influential politicians, bureaucrats, and military officials secured flats in the society by manipulating eligibility criteria and clearances.

Nirav Modi PNB Scam (2018):

The Nirav Modi Punjab National Bank (PNB) scam involved fraudulent transactions and letters of undertaking, leading to a massive financial fraud in one of India's largest public sector banks. Nirav Modi, a prominent jeweler, and his associates were accused of orchestrating the scam.

Sterlite Copper Smelter Plant Protests (2018):

The protests against the Sterlite Copper smelter plant in Thoothukudi, Tamil Nadu, were sparked by allegations of environmental violations and corruption in obtaining permits. The protests turned violent, resulting in several deaths and injuries.

Saradha Group Chit Fund Scam (2013):

The Saradha Group chit fund scam was a financial fraud that affected several states in India, primarily West Bengal. The group collected deposits from investors promising high returns but ultimately defaulted, resulting in significant losses for investors. Prominent politicians and leaders of the Saradha Group faced charges in this case.

These high-profile corporate corruption cases in India have underscored the need for transparency, accountability, and stringent regulatory measures to combat corruption and unethical practices within the corporate and government sectors. They have also led to calls for reforms and increased vigilance in addressing corruption at various levels of society.

CHAPTER FIVE
Corruption in Law Enforcement

Discussing the Challenges of Corruption within Law Enforcement Agencies

Corruption within law enforcement agencies represents a significant threat to public trust, safety, and the rule of law. In this chapter, we explore the complex issue of corruption in law enforcement, examining its various forms, root causes, consequences, and strategies for prevention and mitigation.

5.1 Forms of Corruption in Law Enforcement

5.1.1 Bribery

Bribery in law enforcement occurs when officers accept money, gifts, or favors in exchange for special treatment, ignoring criminal activities, or providing confidential information.

5.1.2 Extortion

Extortion involves officers using their authority to threaten or coerce individuals into paying bribes or providing other benefits to avoid legal action or harassment.

5.1.3 Embezzlement

Embezzlement within law enforcement agencies refers to officers misappropriating funds or property seized during investigations, diverting them for personal gain.

5.1.4 Drug Trafficking and Smuggling

Some law enforcement officers become involved in drug trafficking and smuggling, using their positions to facilitate illegal drug activities.

5.1.5 Evidence Tampering

Evidence tampering involves officers altering or destroying evidence to manipulate the outcome of investigations or legal proceedings.

5.2 Causes of Corruption in Law Enforcement

5.2.1 Low Salaries and Financial Stress

Low salaries and financial stress can make law enforcement personnel susceptible to corruption when they struggle to meet their financial needs.

5.2.2 Lack of Accountability

A lack of accountability and transparency within law enforcement agencies can create an environment where corrupt practices go unchecked.

5.2.3 Organizational Culture

An organizational culture that tolerates or ignores corruption can foster a climate where unethical behavior among officers is normalized.

5.2.4 Limited Oversight

Limited oversight and internal checks and balances can enable corrupt officers to operate without detection.

5.3 Consequences of Corruption in Law Enforcement

5.3.1 Erosion of Public Trust

Corruption in law enforcement erodes public trust, reducing cooperation with police and diminishing confidence in the criminal justice system.

5.3.2 Compromised Investigations

Corrupt practices compromise investigations and undermine the pursuit of justice, potentially leading to wrongful convictions or acquittals.

5.3.3 Impunity and Injustice

Corrupt officers may engage in unjust actions, including abuse of power, wrongful arrests, and excessive use of force, with little fear of consequences.

5.3.4 Undermining the Rule of Law

Corruption within law enforcement agencies weakens the rule of law, eroding the foundations of a just and equitable society.

5.4 Strategies for Prevention and Mitigation

5.4.1 Strong Internal Oversight

Law enforcement agencies should establish robust internal oversight mechanisms to monitor officer conduct and ensure accountability.

5.4.2 Adequate Salaries and Benefits

Ensuring that law enforcement personnel receive competitive salaries and benefits can reduce financial stress and the temptation to engage in corrupt practices.

5.4.3 Whistleblower Protection

Whistleblower protection laws and mechanisms should be in place to encourage officers to report corruption without fear of retaliation.

5.4.4 Ethical Training and Education

Ongoing training and education on ethics and integrity can help instill a culture of accountability within law enforcement agencies.

5.4.5 Community Engagement

Building positive relationships and trust between law enforcement agencies and the communities they serve can deter corruption and enhance accountability.

5.5 Conclusion

Corruption within law enforcement agencies is a complex challenge that demands proactive measures to prevent and address it. By addressing root causes, fostering transparency, and promoting a culture of integrity, law enforcement agencies can uphold their essential role in maintaining justice and public safety while ensuring the trust of the communities they serve.

Exploring the Complex Issues of Police Misconduct and Abuse of Power

Police misconduct and abuse of power are critical issues that challenge the integrity of law enforcement agencies and erode public trust. In this chapter, we delve into the multifaceted nature of police misconduct, its various manifestations, underlying causes, consequences, and strategies for prevention and accountability.

6.1 Forms of Police Misconduct and Abuse of Power

6.1.1 Excessive Use of Force

Excessive use of force involves the unjustified or disproportionate use of physical force by police officers during encounters with civilians, resulting in injury or death.

6.1.2 Racial Profiling

Racial profiling occurs when law enforcement officers target individuals based on their race, ethnicity, or other protected characteristics rather than on objective evidence of wrongdoing.

6.1.3 Unlawful Arrests and Detentions

Police misconduct may include making unlawful arrests or detentions without proper legal justification or due process.

6.1.4 Corruption and Bribery

Some police officers engage in corrupt practices, such as accepting bribes, engaging in drug trafficking, or extorting money from individuals or businesses.

6.1.5 Evidence Tampering and False Testimony

Misconduct can involve tampering with evidence or providing false testimony in criminal investigations or court proceedings, undermining the pursuit of justice.

6.2 Causes of Police Misconduct and Abuse of Power

6.2.1 Lack of Accountability

A lack of accountability mechanisms and transparency within law enforcement agencies can embolden officers to engage in misconduct without fear of consequences.

6.2.2 Inadequate Training

Insufficient training on de-escalation techniques, cultural sensitivity, and ethical behavior can contribute to inappropriate conduct by police officers.

6.2.3 Institutional Culture

An organizational culture that tolerates misconduct or prioritizes quotas and performance metrics over ethical behavior can foster a climate of abuse.

6.2.4 Implicit Bias

Implicit bias, or unconscious prejudices, can influence police interactions and contribute to racial profiling and discriminatory practices.

6.3 Consequences of Police Misconduct and Abuse of Power

6.3.1 Erosion of Public Trust

Police misconduct damages public trust and undermines the legitimacy of law enforcement agencies, making it more challenging for officers to effectively serve and protect communities.

6.3.2 Social Unrest

High-profile cases of police misconduct can lead to social unrest, protests, and calls for justice, resulting in public demonstrations and potential civil disturbances.

6.3.3 Legal and Financial Liability

Misconduct allegations can lead to legal and financial liabilities for law enforcement agencies, which may face lawsuits, settlements, or judgments.

6.3.4 Harm to Communities

Police misconduct can result in physical harm, emotional trauma, and distrust within affected communities, particularly marginalized or minority groups.

6.4 Strategies for Prevention and Accountability

6.4.1 Body-Worn Cameras

Body-worn cameras can provide transparency and accountability by recording interactions between police officers and civilians, serving as a deterrent against misconduct.

6.4.2 Independent Oversight

Establishing independent oversight bodies or civilian review boards can help investigate and address allegations of police misconduct.

6.4.3 Training and Cultural Change

Comprehensive training programs that emphasize de-escalation, cultural competence, and ethical conduct can promote responsible policing.

6.4.4 Whistleblower Protection

Strong whistleblower protection laws can encourage officers to report misconduct without fear of retaliation.

6.4.5 Community Policing

Emphasizing community policing approaches that build positive relationships and trust between law enforcement agencies and communities can reduce incidents of misconduct.

6.5 Conclusion

Addressing police misconduct and abuse of power is crucial for ensuring justice, public safety, and trust in law enforcement. It requires a multifaceted approach that includes accountability mechanisms, improved training, and meaningful engagement with affected communities to prevent and rectify instances of misconduct and abuse.

Strategies and Initiatives to Tackle Corruption in Law Enforcement

Effectively combating corruption within the police force is essential to uphold the rule of law, ensure public trust, and promote ethical policing. In this chapter, we explore the various strategies and initiatives aimed at addressing and preventing corruption within law enforcement agencies.

7.1 Strengthening Accountability Mechanisms

7.1.1 Independent Oversight Bodies

Establishing independent oversight bodies or civilian review boards tasked with investigating allegations of police misconduct can provide transparency and impartiality in the review process.

7.1.2 Internal Affairs Units

Empowering internal affairs units within law enforcement agencies to investigate allegations of corruption and misconduct among their peers is crucial for maintaining accountability.

7.1.3 Whistleblower Protection

Enacting robust whistleblower protection laws and mechanisms can encourage police officers to report corrupt practices without fear of retaliation.

7.1.4 Transparency and Reporting

Implementing transparent reporting mechanisms for misconduct complaints, investigations, and outcomes can build public trust and accountability.

7.2 Enhanced Training and Education

7.2.1 Ethical Training

Incorporating ethics and integrity training into the curriculum for police recruits and ongoing professional development programs can reinforce ethical behavior.

7.2.2 De-Escalation Techniques

Providing comprehensive training in de-escalation techniques and conflict resolution can help officers handle difficult situations without resorting to excessive force.

7.2.3 Cultural Sensitivity

Promoting cultural sensitivity and diversity training can reduce incidents of racial profiling and discriminatory practices.

7.2.4 Use of Technology

Utilizing technology, such as body-worn cameras and data analysis tools, can help monitor police conduct and provide valuable evidence in cases of misconduct.

7.3 Community Engagement

7.3.1 Community Policing

Emphasizing community policing approaches that foster positive relationships and trust between officers and the communities they serve can prevent corruption and misconduct.

7.3.2 Citizen Oversight

Engaging the community in oversight and accountability processes can ensure that police officers are held accountable for their actions.

7.3.3 Outreach and Education

Conducting outreach programs and educational initiatives to inform citizens about their rights and how to file complaints can empower the public to report misconduct.

7.4 Legal and Policy Reforms

7.4.1 Zero Tolerance Policies

Implementing and enforcing zero tolerance policies for corruption and misconduct sends a strong message that such behavior will not be tolerated.

7.4.2 Anti-Corruption Legislation

Enacting and enforcing anti-corruption legislation specific to law enforcement can provide a legal framework for addressing and preventing corrupt practices.

7.4.3 Asset Forfeiture Laws

Asset forfeiture laws can allow authorities to seize assets acquired through corrupt means, providing a financial disincentive for corruption.

7.4.4 Body-Worn Cameras

Mandating the use of body-worn cameras by police officers during interactions with the public can increase transparency and accountability.

7.5 Conclusion

Efforts to combat corruption within the police force require a comprehensive and multi-faceted approach that addresses root causes, strengthens accountability mechanisms, and fosters a culture of integrity and transparency. By implementing these strategies and initiatives, law enforcement agencies can work toward restoring public trust and ensuring ethical policing practices.

CHAPTER SIX

The Role of Money Laundering

Exploring How Money Laundering Facilitates Corruption

Money laundering plays a pivotal role in facilitating and perpetuating corruption across the globe. In this chapter, we delve into the intricate web of money laundering, its connections to corruption, and the devastating consequences it has on societies, economies, and the rule of law.

6.1 Understanding Money Laundering

6.1.1 Money Laundering Defined

Money laundering is the process by which illicitly obtained funds, often from criminal activities such as corruption, bribery, drug trafficking, or fraud, are concealed and integrated into the legitimate financial system to make them appear legal and clean.

6.1.2 The Money Laundering Cycle

Money laundering typically involves three stages: placement (introducing dirty money into the financial system), layering (creating complex transactions to obscure the source), and integration (making the money appear legitimate).

6.1.3 Methods of Money Laundering

Money launderers employ various methods, including shell companies, offshore accounts, real estate investments, and trade-based laundering, to legitimize illicit funds.

6.2 The Interplay Between Money Laundering and Corruption

6.2.1 Corrupt Funds as the Source

Money laundering often begins with corrupt funds, as individuals and entities seek to hide the proceeds of corruption, bribery, or embezzlement.

6.2.2 Protecting Ill-Gotten Gains

Money laundering shields corrupt officials and individuals from legal scrutiny by making it difficult to trace and seize their ill-gotten gains.

6.2.3 Sustaining Corruption Networks

Money laundering helps sustain corrupt networks by allowing the flow of funds to continue corrupt practices, undermining the rule of law and the fight against corruption.

6.2.4 Financing Criminal Enterprises

Laundered funds may also finance other criminal activities, including organized crime, terrorism, and drug trafficking, further exacerbating the harm caused by corruption.

6.3 Consequences of Money Laundering

6.3.1 Erosion of Trust

Money laundering erodes public trust in financial institutions, governments, and the legal system, as it creates a perception that corruption goes unchecked.

6.3.2 Economic Damage

Money laundering distorts markets, inflates asset prices, and leads to misallocation of resources, ultimately harming the economy.

6.3.3 Legal and Regulatory Responses

Governments must invest significant resources in combating money laundering, diverting attention and resources from other critical priorities.

6.3.4 Global Implications

Money laundering is a global issue, with the flow of illicit funds often crossing borders, making it a challenge for individual countries to combat effectively.

6.4 Combating Money Laundering and Corruption

6.4.1 Strengthening Anti-Money Laundering (AML) Laws

Governments must enact and enforce robust AML laws to detect and deter money laundering, particularly when linked to corruption.

6.4.2 Enhanced Financial Transparency

Promoting financial transparency through measures like beneficial ownership registries can make it more difficult for corrupt individuals to hide behind anonymous entities.

6.4.3 International Cooperation

Enhanced international cooperation and information sharing are essential for tracking and seizing laundered assets that cross borders.

6.4.4 Civil Society and Whistleblower Protections

Civil society organizations and whistleblower protections play a vital role in exposing money laundering and corruption and holding perpetrators accountable.

6.5 Conclusion

Money laundering is a critical enabler of corruption, allowing corrupt individuals and entities to reap the benefits of their illicit activities while evading justice. To combat corruption effectively, it is imperative to address money laundering through comprehensive legal, regulatory, and international efforts that promote transparency, accountability, and the rule of law.

Uncovering the Elaborate Methods Employed to Cleanse Illicit Funds

Money laundering is a clandestine and intricate process employed to legitimize illegally acquired proceeds. In this chapter, we explore the techniques and methods commonly used in money laundering, shedding light on the tactics that corrupt individuals and criminal organizations utilize to conceal their ill-gotten gains.

7.1 Placement: Introducing Dirty Money into the Financial System

7.1.1 Smurfing

Smurfing involves breaking down large sums of illicit money into smaller, less suspicious amounts to deposit into financial institutions, thereby avoiding suspicion and reporting requirements.

7.1.2 Structuring or Layering Deposits

Money launderers may make multiple small deposits into bank accounts or use various financial instruments to create complex transaction patterns, making it difficult to trace the origin of funds.

7.1.3 Cash Businesses

Money launderers may set up cash-based businesses, such as restaurants or casinos, where illicit funds can be mingled with legitimate revenue.

7.1.4 Underground Banking

Underground or informal banking systems, often known as hawala or black market peso exchange, facilitate the transfer of funds without a formal paper trail.

7.2 Layering: Creating Complex Transactions to Obscure the Source

7.2.1 Shell Companies

Money launderers establish shell companies, often in offshore jurisdictions, to create a complex network of transactions that mask the origin of funds.

7.2.2 Real Estate Investments

Illicit funds can be used to purchase real estate, making it difficult to trace the source of wealth and providing a safe haven for money laundering.

7.2.3 Trade-Based Money Laundering

Criminal organizations may manipulate trade transactions by over- or under-invoicing goods, enabling the movement of funds across borders while disguising their true purpose.

7.2.4 Digital Currencies

Cryptocurrencies can be used to launder money due to their pseudonymous nature, allowing criminals to move funds with relative anonymity.

7.3 Integration: Making Illicit Funds Appear Legitimate

7.3.1 Investing in Legitimate Assets

Money launderers invest in legitimate assets, such as stocks, businesses, or luxury goods, to give the appearance of lawful wealth.

7.3.2 Repatriation of Funds

Funds may be repatriated into the legitimate financial system as clean assets, further obscuring their illicit origins.

7.3.3 Shell Company Dissolution

Money launderers may dissolve shell companies, converting their assets into seemingly legitimate assets while eliminating the trail.

7.3.4 Offshore Banking

Offshore accounts can be used to repatriate funds or maintain wealth in jurisdictions with strict banking secrecy laws.

7.4 Technological Advances and Money Laundering

7.4.1 Use of Cryptocurrencies

Cryptocurrencies provide new opportunities for money launderers to transfer and launder funds while evading traditional financial institutions.

7.4.2 Digital Payment Systems

Digital payment platforms and peer-to-peer transfers can be exploited for money laundering purposes.

7.5 The Role of Financial Institutions

7.5.1 Compliance and Due Diligence

Financial institutions are key players in the fight against money laundering and are required to implement robust compliance measures and due diligence procedures.

7.5.2 Regulatory Reporting

Banks and financial institutions must report suspicious transactions to regulatory authorities to aid in the detection and prevention of money laundering.

7.6 Conclusion

Money laundering techniques continue to evolve, presenting challenges for law enforcement and regulatory authorities worldwide.

Understanding these methods is crucial for combating money laundering effectively and disrupting the financial infrastructure that sustains corruption and criminal enterprises.

Exploring the Complex Interplay Between Illicit Funds and Corrupt Activities

The connection between dirty money and corrupt practices is a multifaceted issue with far-reaching implications for societies, economies, and the rule of law. In this chapter, we delve into the intricate relationship between funds obtained through corruption and the corrupt activities that generate and utilize this ill-gotten wealth.

8.1 Defining Dirty Money

8.1.1 Dirty Money Defined

Dirty money encompasses funds acquired through illegal or unethical means, such as corruption, bribery, embezzlement, fraud, drug trafficking, and other criminal activities.

8.1.2 Proceeds of Corruption

A significant portion of dirty money consists of proceeds generated from corrupt practices within both the public and private sectors.

8.2 The Sources of Dirty Money: Corrupt Practices

8.2.1 Corruption in Government

Corrupt practices within government institutions, such as bribery, embezzlement, and kickbacks, generate substantial dirty money.

8.2.2 Corporate Corruption

Corrupt activities in the corporate world, including fraud, accounting manipulation, and unethical business practices, contribute to the flow of illicit funds.

8.2.3 Organized Crime

Organized crime networks engage in various criminal enterprises, such as drug trafficking, human smuggling, and extortion, generating significant dirty money.

8.2.4 Money Laundering as a Facilitator

Money laundering serves as a critical enabler, allowing corrupt individuals and organizations to cleanse and legitimize their ill-gotten wealth.

8.3 The Impact of Dirty Money on Society and Governance

8.3.1 Erosion of Trust

The prevalence of dirty money erodes public trust in institutions and undermines confidence in governments, businesses, and the rule of law.

8.3.2 Impunity and Injustice

The flow of dirty money can perpetuate a culture of impunity, allowing corrupt individuals and entities to evade justice for their actions.

8.3.3 Economic Distortion

Dirty money distorts markets, drives up asset prices, and results in economic misallocation, harming legitimate businesses and investors.

8.3.4 Inequality and Social Harm

The concentration of wealth generated through corrupt practices exacerbates economic inequality and can lead to social unrest and instability.

8.4 Combating the Connection Between Dirty Money and Corruption

8.4.1 Legal and Regulatory Frameworks

Strengthening anti-corruption laws and regulations and enhancing enforcement mechanisms are essential steps in tackling the connection between dirty money and corruption.

8.4.2 Financial Transparency

Promoting financial transparency through measures like beneficial ownership registries can make it more challenging for corrupt individuals and entities to hide their assets.

8.4.3 International Cooperation

Enhanced international cooperation and information sharing are critical for tracking and seizing dirty money that flows across borders.

8.4.4 Civil Society and Whistleblower Protections

Civil society organizations and whistleblower protections play a vital role in exposing corrupt practices and holding perpetrators accountable.

8.5 Conclusion

The connection between dirty money and corrupt practices is a pervasive challenge that demands comprehensive efforts to combat corruption at its roots. By addressing the sources of dirty money, enhancing transparency, and promoting accountability, societies can work toward a more just and equitable future free from the corrosive effects of corruption.

CHAPTER SEVEN
International Corruption

Examining the Global Efforts Led by International Organizations to Tackle Corruption

International organizations play a crucial role in combating corruption on a global scale. In this chapter, we explore the multifaceted contributions and initiatives led by international bodies to address corruption, foster transparency, and promote good governance worldwide.

9.1 Defining International Organizations

9.1.1 International Organizations Defined

International organizations are entities formed by multiple nations to foster cooperation and address global issues collectively. They can include intergovernmental organizations, non-governmental organizations (NGOs), and regional entities.

9.1.2 Key International Organizations in Anti-Corruption Efforts

Notable international organizations engaged in anti-corruption efforts include the United Nations (UN), World Bank, International Monetary

Fund (IMF), Transparency International, and regional bodies like the African Union (AU) and the Organization of American States (OAS).

9.2 The Global Impact of Corruption

9.2.1 The Cost of Corruption

Corruption poses significant economic, social, and political costs, affecting countries' development, stability, and the well-being of their citizens.

9.2.2 Transnational Nature of Corruption

Corruption often transcends national borders, making it a global issue that necessitates international cooperation.

9.3 The Role of International Organizations in Combating Corruption

9.3.1 Establishing Anti-Corruption Conventions

International organizations have played a pivotal role in creating anti-corruption conventions and agreements, such as the United Nations Convention against Corruption (UNCAC), which set global standards for combating corruption.

9.3.2 Technical Assistance and Capacity Building

Many international organizations provide technical assistance and capacity-building programs to help countries develop effective anti-corruption strategies, institutions, and legislation.

9.3.3 Research and Data Collection

Organizations like Transparency International conduct research and collect data on corruption levels globally, providing valuable insights into corruption trends and challenges.

9.3.4 Advocacy and Awareness

International organizations engage in advocacy efforts to raise awareness about the detrimental effects of corruption and encourage governments and civil society to take action.

9.3.5 Monitoring and Reporting

Bodies like the UN and regional organizations monitor compliance with anti-corruption conventions and report on progress and challenges in individual countries.

9.4 Regional Anti-Corruption Initiatives

9.4.1 Regional Bodies

Regional organizations, such as the European Union (EU), AU, and OAS, have launched their anti-corruption initiatives and mechanisms to address corruption specific to their regions.

9.4.2 Exchange of Best Practices

Regional anti-corruption initiatives facilitate the exchange of best practices among member countries, helping to tailor solutions to regional contexts.

9.5 Challenges and Limitations

9.5.1 Political Will

The effectiveness of international efforts to combat corruption depends on the political will of individual governments to implement anti-corruption measures.

9.5.2 Enforcement and Compliance

Ensuring that countries enforce anti-corruption laws and comply with international agreements remains a challenge.

9.5.3 Resource Constraints

Many countries, particularly those with limited resources, face challenges in implementing robust anti-corruption measures.

9.6 Conclusion

International organizations play a critical role in fostering a coordinated global response to corruption. Through conventions, technical assistance, research, and advocacy, these organizations contribute to the collective effort to combat corruption, promote good governance, and create a more just and equitable world. However, the fight against corruption remains an ongoing and complex challenge that requires sustained commitment and collaboration at all levels.

Certainly, there have been numerous notable international corruption scandals that have garnered significant attention and had far-reaching consequences. Here are some of the notable international corruption scandals:

1MDB Scandal (Malaysia, 2015):

The 1Malaysia Development Berhad (1MDB) scandal involved allegations of embezzlement and misappropriation of billions of dollars from a Malaysian government-owned investment fund. The scandal implicated former Malaysian Prime Minister Najib Razak and led to investigations in several countries.

Petrobras Scandal (Brazil, 2014):

The Petrobras scandal, also known as Operation Car Wash, exposed widespread corruption within Brazil's state-owned oil company, Petrobras. High-ranking politicians, business leaders, and executives were implicated in a massive bribery and kickback scheme.

Operation Lava Jato (Brazil, 2014):

Operation Lava Jato was an expansive investigation into corruption and money laundering involving numerous Brazilian politicians and business leaders. It had far-reaching implications and led to the impeachment of President Dilma Rousseff.

Panama Papers (2016):

The Panama Papers leak revealed a global network of offshore tax havens and shell companies used by politicians, celebrities, and business leaders to conceal their wealth and evade taxes. The leak exposed the extent of financial secrecy and tax avoidance schemes.

Gupta Family Scandal (South Africa, 2017):

The Gupta family, with close ties to former South African President Jacob Zuma, was implicated in alleged corruption involving state-owned enterprises and government contracts. The scandal raised concerns about state capture and led to political turmoil in South Africa.

Operation Carne Fraca (Brazil, 2017):

Operation Carne Fraca uncovered corruption in Brazil's meatpacking industry, with accusations of bribes paid to government inspectors in exchange for overlooking unsanitary practices. The scandal had international implications due to Brazil's role as a major meat exporter.

Unaoil Scandal (Global, 2016):

The Unaoil scandal involved a global network of corruption in the oil and gas industry, with allegations of bribes paid to secure contracts in numerous countries. Several major multinational companies were implicated.

Siemens Bribery Scandal (Germany, 2008):

Siemens, one of the world's largest engineering and electronics companies, was embroiled in a massive bribery scandal. The company faced allegations of paying bribes to win contracts in various countries, resulting in a significant settlement and penalties.

Bribery Scandal at Olympus (Japan, 2011):

The Olympus bribery scandal involved allegations of covering up massive investment losses through questionable M&A deals and paying large sums to organized crime groups. The scandal rocked the Japanese corporate world and led to the resignation of top executives.

These international corruption scandals have underscored the need for increased transparency, stronger anti-corruption measures, and international cooperation in combating corrupt practices that can have far-reaching economic, political, and social repercussions.

CHAPTER EIGHT

The Impact on Society

Discussing the Far-Reaching Consequences of Corruption

Corruption exerts profound and far-reaching consequences on societies, affecting not only their economic well-being but also their political stability, social cohesion, and overall development. In this chapter, we delve into the multifaceted impacts of corruption, shedding light on the myriad ways it undermines progress and erodes trust in institutions.

10.1 Economic Consequences

10.1.1 Reduced Economic Growth

Corruption impedes economic growth by distorting markets, deterring investment, and diverting resources away from productive uses.

10.1.2   Inefficient   Resource Allocation

Resources may be misallocated as a result of corrupt practices, preventing them from being directed toward areas of genuine need.

10.1.3 Weakened Investment Climate

A corrupt environment discourages foreign and domestic investment, hindering job creation and economic development.

10.1.4 Income Inequality

Corruption often exacerbates income inequality, as the benefits of corrupt practices tend to accrue to a select few, while the broader population suffers.

10.2 Political Consequences

10.2.1 Erosion of Trust in Institutions

Corruption erodes public trust in government institutions, diminishing their legitimacy and fostering cynicism.

10.2.2 Undermining Democratic Processes

Corrupt practices can distort electoral processes and undermine the principles of democracy, leading to political instability and disenfranchisement.

10.2.3 Encouraging Authoritarianism

In some cases, corruption can lead to the rise of authoritarian leaders who promise to combat corruption but may concentrate power and undermine democratic institutions.

10.2.4 Threats to National Security

Corruption within security and law enforcement agencies can compromise national security, as it may enable criminal enterprises and terrorist organizations to operate with impunity.

10.3 Social Consequences

10.3.1 Impunity and Injustice

Corrupt practices can result in impunity for wrongdoers, leading to injustices, human rights abuses, and a breakdown of the rule of law.

10.3.2 Reduced Access to Public Services

Corruption can limit access to essential public services such as healthcare, education, and clean water, disproportionately affecting marginalized populations.

10.3.3 Social Cohesion

Corruption can erode social cohesion by creating divisions within society, pitting corrupt elites against the rest of the population.

10.3.4 Effects on Vulnerable Groups

Vulnerable and marginalized groups often bear the brunt of corruption's consequences, facing greater barriers to justice and opportunities.

10.4 Global Implications

10.4.1 Transnational Impact

Corruption frequently crosses borders, affecting not only individual nations but also global stability and cooperation.

10.4.2 International Reputation

Countries with high levels of corruption may face reputational damage, hindering their ability to engage in international trade, diplomacy, and partnerships.

10.4.3 Development Challenges

Corruption can impede progress toward achieving the United Nations Sustainable Development Goals (SDGs), exacerbating poverty, inequality, and environmental degradation.

10.5 Combating Corruption for a Better Future

10.5.1 Strengthening Anti-Corruption Measures

Implementing and enforcing robust anti-corruption laws and mechanisms is essential to combat the multifaceted impacts of corruption.

10.5.2 Promoting Transparency and Accountability

Fostering a culture of transparency, accountability, and good governance is crucial to rebuild trust in institutions and mitigate the consequences of corruption.

10.5.3 Empowering Civil Society

Civil society organizations and whistleblower protections play a vital role in exposing corruption and holding wrongdoers accountable.

10.5.4 International Cooperation

Enhanced international cooperation and information sharing are necessary to combat cross-border corruption and its global implications.

10.6 Conclusion

The consequences of corruption are pervasive and far-reaching, touching every aspect of society. Addressing corruption's impacts requires collective action, strong political will, and a commitment to upholding the principles of transparency, accountability, and the rule of law. By combatting corruption, societies can work toward a more just, equitable, and prosperous future for all.

Exploring the Destructive Influence of Corruption on Society

Corruption exerts a corrosive influence on economic development, social stability, and public trust. In this chapter, we examine how corruption undermines these critical pillars of society, hindering progress and eroding the foundations of prosperous and stable nations.

11.1 Corruption's Effect on Economic Development

11.1.1 Reduced Economic Growth

Corruption distorts economic markets, discourages foreign and domestic investment, and hinders economic growth by diverting resources away from productive uses.

11.1.2 Misallocation of Resources

Resources may be misallocated as a result of corrupt practices, leading to inefficient allocation and missed opportunities for development.

11.1.3 Erosion of Business Confidence

Corrupt environments deter business confidence, making it more difficult for companies to operate and expand, limiting job creation and economic prosperity.

11.1.4 Income Inequality

Corruption can exacerbate income inequality as the benefits of corrupt practices often accrue to a privileged few, further dividing society.

11.2 Corruption's Impact on Social Stability

11.2.1 Erosion of Public Trust

Corruption erodes public trust in government institutions, diminishing their legitimacy and fostering cynicism among citizens.

11.2.2 Undermining Democratic Processes

Corrupt practices can distort electoral processes, undermine democratic principles, and lead to political instability.

11.2.3 Encouragement of Authoritarianism

In some cases, corruption can lead to the rise of authoritarian leaders who promise to combat corruption but may concentrate power and weaken democratic institutions.

11.2.4 Threats to National Security

Corruption within security and law enforcement agencies can compromise national security, allowing criminal enterprises and terrorist organizations to operate with impunity.

11.3 Corruption's Impact on Public Trust

11.3.1 Impunity and Injustice

Corruption can lead to a culture of impunity, where wrongdoers escape justice, resulting in injustices, human rights abuses, and a breakdown of the rule of law.

11.3.2 Reduced Access to Public Services

Corruption limits access to essential public services, disproportionately affecting marginalized populations and exacerbating social inequalities.

11.3.3 Erosion of Social Cohesion

Corruption can erode social cohesion by creating divisions within society, pitting corrupt elites against the rest of the population.

11.3.4 Effects on Vulnerable Groups

Vulnerable and marginalized groups often bear the brunt of corruption's consequences, facing greater barriers to justice and opportunities.

11.4 The Vicious Cycle of Corruption

11.4.1 A Self-Perpetuating Problem

Corruption often becomes a self-perpetuating problem, as corrupt individuals and institutions work to protect their interests and maintain the status quo.

11.4.2 The Role of Enablers

Enablers of corruption, including those who provide bribes or fail to report corrupt practices, contribute to the perpetuation of this destructive cycle.

11.5 Combating Corruption for Progress and Stability

11.5.1 Strengthening Anti-Corruption Measures

Implementing and enforcing robust anti-corruption laws and mechanisms is essential to break the cycle of corruption and promote progress.

11.5.2 Promoting Transparency and Accountability

Fostering a culture of transparency, accountability, and good governance is crucial to rebuild public trust and mitigate the consequences of corruption.

11.5.3 Empowering Civil Society

Civil society organizations and whistleblower protections play a vital role in exposing corruption and holding wrongdoers accountable.

11.5.4 International Cooperation

Enhanced international cooperation and information sharing are necessary to combat cross-border corruption and its global implications.

11.6 Conclusion

Corruption's impact on economic development, social stability, and public trust is profound and damaging. Addressing corruption is not only a moral imperative but also a pragmatic necessity for societies to achieve sustainable development, political stability, and a brighter future for all.

Exploring the Profound Toll Corruption Takes on Individuals and Communities

Corruption exacts a heavy human toll, affecting individuals and communities in myriad ways. In this chapter, we delve into the deeply personal and far-reaching consequences of corruption on the lives of people, their access to basic rights and services, and their overall well-being.

12.1 Denied Access to Basic Services

12.1.1 Healthcare

Corruption in healthcare systems can result in inadequate medical care, lack of access to essential medicines, and compromised health outcomes for individuals.

12.1.2 Education

Corrupt practices in education systems may lead to unequal access to quality education, limiting opportunities for personal growth and socio-economic advancement.

12.1.3 Clean Water and Sanitation

Corruption can impede efforts to provide clean water and sanitation, leading to waterborne diseases and undermining public health.

12.1.4 Housing and Infrastructure

Corrupt allocation of housing and infrastructure projects can leave communities without safe and adequate housing, reliable transportation, and other essential amenities.

12.2 Erosion of Trust and Justice

12.2.1 Public Trust

Corruption erodes public trust in government institutions, fostering disillusionment and diminishing citizens' belief in the fairness and efficacy of their systems.

12.2.2 Impunity and Injustice

A culture of corruption can lead to impunity, allowing wrongdoers to escape justice and perpetuating a sense of injustice within society.

12.2.3 Human Rights Abuses

Corruption can lead to human rights abuses, as individuals with power and resources exploit their positions at the expense of vulnerable populations.

12.3 Economic Hardships and Poverty

12.3.1 Income Inequality

Corruption often exacerbates income inequality, concentrating wealth in the hands of a few while leaving many in poverty.

12.3.2 Job Losses and Economic Disruptions

Economic instability resulting from corruption can lead to job losses, inflation, and economic hardships for individuals and families.

12.3.3 Stunted Economic Development

Corruption hampers economic development, limiting opportunities for entrepreneurship and impeding progress in developing countries.

12.4 Health and Well-Being

12.4.1 Mental Health Impacts

The stress, frustration, and hopelessness stemming from corruption can have detrimental effects on individuals' mental health and overall well-being.

12.4.2 Reduced Life Expectancy

Corruption's impact on healthcare and public services can lead to reduced life expectancy and lower quality of life for individuals in affected regions.

12.4.3 Food Insecurity

Corruption in food distribution and agricultural systems can result in food insecurity and malnutrition, particularly among vulnerable populations.

12.5 Vulnerable Groups and Marginalization

12.5.1 Disproportionate Effects

Vulnerable and marginalized groups, such as women, minorities, and the poor, often bear the brunt of corruption's consequences, facing greater barriers to justice and opportunities.

12.5.2 Human Trafficking and Exploitation

Corruption can facilitate human trafficking and exploitation, leaving individuals vulnerable to forced labor, sexual exploitation, and other forms of abuse.

12.6 Combating Corruption to Alleviate Human Suffering

12.6.1 Empowering Civil Society

Civil society organizations and grassroots movements play a vital role in raising awareness, advocating for change, and holding corrupt actors accountable.

12.6.2 Strengthening Anti-Corruption Measures

Implementing and enforcing robust anti-corruption laws and mechanisms is essential to alleviate the human cost of corruption.

12.6.3 International Cooperation

Enhanced international cooperation and information sharing are necessary to combat cross-border corruption and protect vulnerable populations.

12.7 Conclusion

The human cost of corruption is immeasurable, affecting the lives and well-being of countless individuals and communities worldwide. Addressing corruption is not only a matter of ethics but also a fundamental imperative to alleviate human suffering, promote justice, and create a more equitable and prosperous world for all.

CHAPTER NINE
Fighting Corruption
Highlighting Efforts and Strategies to Combat Corruption

Efforts to combat corruption are essential to fostering transparency, accountability, and good governance. In this chapter, we explore various strategies and initiatives aimed at addressing corruption at local, national, and international levels, as well as the role of individuals, civil society, and governments in the fight against corruption.

13.1 Legal and Regulatory Frameworks

13.1.1 Strengthening Anti-Corruption Laws

Governments can enact and enforce comprehensive anti-corruption laws that criminalize corrupt practices, establish penalties, and provide avenues for reporting corruption.

13.1.2 Whistleblower Protections

Whistleblower protection laws can encourage individuals to come forward with information about corrupt activities without fear of retaliation.

13.1.3 Asset Recovery Mechanisms

Asset recovery laws and international cooperation agreements enable the seizure and repatriation of ill-gotten assets obtained through corruption.

13.2 Institutional Reforms

13.2.1 Independent Anti-Corruption Agencies

Establishing independent anti-corruption agencies can enhance the effectiveness of anti-corruption efforts by investigating and prosecuting corruption cases.

13.2.2 Transparent Procurement Processes

Transparent procurement and contracting processes reduce the opportunities for corruption in public procurement.

13.2.3 Strengthened Judiciary

An independent and robust judiciary is essential for ensuring that corrupt individuals face legal consequences for their actions.

13.3 Promoting Transparency and Accountability

13.3.1 Open Data and Access to Information

Governments can promote transparency by making data and information related to public finances, contracts, and government activities accessible to the public.

13.3.2 Whistleblower Hotlines

Establishing whistleblower hotlines allows individuals to report corruption anonymously and confidentially.

13.3.3 Beneficial Ownership Registries

Beneficial ownership registries disclose the true owners of companies and assets, reducing opportunities for hiding corrupt proceeds.

13.4 International Cooperation

13.4.1 United Nations Convention against Corruption (UNCAC)

The UNCAC provides a framework for international cooperation in combating corruption, promoting the exchange of information and best practices.

13.4.2 Mutual Legal Assistance Treaties (MLATs)

MLATs facilitate cooperation among countries in investigating and prosecuting cross-border corruption cases.

13.4.3 Global Anti-Corruption Initiatives

Organizations like Transparency International and the World Bank support global anti-corruption initiatives by conducting research, advocating for reforms, and promoting best practices.

13.5 Civil Society and Public Engagement

13.5.1 Civil Society Organizations (CSOs)

CSOs play a crucial role in monitoring government activities, advocating for anti-corruption measures, and raising awareness about corruption's detrimental effects.

13.5.2 Social Media and Citizen Journalism

Social media and citizen journalism platforms empower individuals to expose corruption and hold public officials accountable.

13.5.3 Public Education Campaigns

Public education campaigns can inform citizens about the consequences of corruption and encourage them to become active participants in anti-corruption efforts.

13.6 Personal Responsibility

13.6.1 Ethical Leadership

Ethical leadership at all levels of society sets a positive example and reinforces the importance of integrity and accountability.

13.6.2 Ethical Consumerism

Consumers can make choices that support ethical businesses and avoid companies associated with corrupt practices.

13.6.3 Community Engagement

Engaging in community initiatives and supporting local governance efforts can promote transparency and accountability at the grassroots level.

13.7 Conclusion

The fight against corruption requires a multifaceted approach that involves individuals, civil society, governments, and international organizations. By implementing legal reforms, enhancing transparency, and promoting accountability, societies can work collectively to combat corruption and build a more just and equitable future for all.

Exploring the Critical Role of Laws and Enforcement Mechanisms in the Fight Against Corruption

Anti-corruption legislation and its effective enforcement are fundamental to combatting corrupt practices and fostering transparency and accountability within society. In this chapter, we delve into the key elements of anti-corruption laws, mechanisms for enforcement, and their impact on eradicating corruption.

14.1 Anti-Corruption Legislation

14.1.1 Defining Corruption Offenses

Anti-corruption laws define various corruption offenses, such as bribery, embezzlement, abuse of power, and money laundering, providing a legal framework to address corrupt practices.

14.1.2 Penalties and Sanctions

These laws establish penalties and sanctions for individuals and entities found guilty of corrupt activities, including fines, imprisonment, and asset forfeiture.

14.1.3 Whistleblower Protections

Legislation often includes provisions to protect whistleblowers who report corruption, safeguarding them from retaliation.

14.1.4 Asset Recovery

Asset recovery provisions empower authorities to identify, freeze, and repatriate assets obtained through corruption, even when located abroad.

14.2 Independent Anti-Corruption Agencies

14.2.1 Formation and Mandate

Many countries establish independent anti-corruption agencies responsible for investigating and prosecuting corruption cases, often with a specific mandate to operate free from political interference.

14.2.2 Powers and Resources

These agencies are typically granted investigative powers and adequate resources to carry out their duties effectively.

14.2.3 Reporting and Transparency

Independent anti-corruption agencies often publish reports on their activities and findings to promote transparency and accountability.

14.3 Law Enforcement and Judicial Measures

14.3.1 Investigative Bodies

Law enforcement agencies and specialized anti-corruption units investigate corruption cases, gather evidence, and build cases for prosecution.

14.3.2 Judicial Independence

An independent judiciary is essential for ensuring that corruption cases are tried fairly and impartially, holding wrongdoers accountable.

14.3.3 International Cooperation

Cooperation between countries and mutual legal assistance treaties (MLATs) facilitate the extradition and prosecution of corrupt individuals across borders.

14.4 Transparency and Access to Information

14.4.1 Freedom of Information Laws

Freedom of information laws promote transparency by granting citizens access to government information and data.

14.4.2 Open Budgeting

Transparent budgeting and financial reporting processes minimize opportunities for corruption in public finances.

14.4.3 Beneficial Ownership Registers

Establishing beneficial ownership registers discloses the true owners of companies and assets, reducing opportunities for corrupt individuals to hide their wealth.

14.5 International Agreements and Conventions

14.5.1 United Nations Convention against Corruption (UNCAC)

The UNCAC provides a global framework for countries to adopt and enforce anti-corruption measures, fostering international cooperation.

14.5.2 Regional Agreements

Regional agreements, such as those within the European Union (EU) or the African Union (AU), promote anti-corruption efforts and cooperation among member states.

14.5.3 Cross-Border Extradition

Agreements on cross-border extradition allow for the prosecution of corrupt individuals who flee to other countries.

14.6 Challenges and Considerations

14.6.1 Political Will

The effectiveness of anti-corruption legislation and enforcement depends on the political will of governments to enforce the laws impartially.

14.6.2 Corruption Within the Judiciary

Corruption within the judiciary can hinder effective enforcement of anti-corruption laws and necessitates measures to ensure judicial integrity.

14.6.3 Civil Society Oversight

Civil society organizations play a crucial role in monitoring and advocating for the effective enforcement of anti-corruption measures.

14.7 Conclusion

Robust anti-corruption legislation and effective enforcement mechanisms are cornerstones of the fight against corruption. By enacting and enforcing anti-corruption laws, empowering independent agencies, promoting transparency, and fostering international cooperation, societies can work toward a future with reduced corruption and increased accountability.

Examining Positive Examples of Anti-Corruption Efforts

While the battle against corruption is ongoing, there are inspiring success stories that highlight the effectiveness of anti-corruption measures. In this chapter, we explore some notable cases where countries, institutions, and individuals have made significant strides in combating corruption and promoting transparency and accountability.

15.1 Singapore: The Lion City's Clean Governance

15.1.1 Transparent Governance

Singapore is celebrated for its transparent and accountable government, with strong anti-corruption laws and institutions in place.

15.1.2 Strict Enforcement

The city-state enforces its anti-corruption laws rigorously, with a zero-tolerance approach that has led to a consistently low level of corruption.

15.1.3 Independent Anti-Corruption Agency

The Corrupt Practices Investigation Bureau (CPIB) operates independently, investigating corruption cases without political interference.

15.1.4 Success in Attracting Investment

Singapore's reputation for clean governance has made it an attractive destination for foreign investment and a global business hub.

15.2 Rwanda: Transformative Progress

15.2.1 Post-Genocide Reforms

Rwanda has undergone significant reforms since the devastating genocide in the 1990s, including anti-corruption initiatives.

15.2.2 E-Government Solutions

The country has embraced technology and e-government solutions to reduce corruption and enhance transparency in public services.

15.2.3 Empowered Women

Rwanda boasts a high representation of women in government, contributing to a more inclusive and accountable political landscape.

15.2.4 Anti-Corruption Courts

Specialized anti-corruption courts have been established to expedite corruption cases, ensuring justice is served promptly.

15.3 Hong Kong: The Independent Commission Against Corruption (ICAC)

15.3.1 Establishment of ICAC

Hong Kong's ICAC, formed in 1974, is renowned for its independence and effectiveness in tackling corruption.

15.3.2 Public Awareness and Education

The ICAC conducts public awareness campaigns and educational programs to promote anti-corruption values.

15.3.3 High-Profile Convictions

The ICAC has successfully prosecuted high-profile corruption cases, sending a strong message that corruption will not be tolerated.

15.4 Georgia: From Corruption Hotspot to Reform Champion

15.4.1 Swift Reforms

Georgia undertook swift and comprehensive reforms to combat corruption and improve governance after the Rose Revolution in 2003.

15.4.2 E-Governance and Simplification

The country introduced e-governance tools and simplified procedures to reduce opportunities for corruption.

15.4.3 Positive Business Climate

These efforts have transformed Georgia into a more attractive destination for business and investment.

15.5 Lessons Learned and Global Impact

15.5.1 The Role of Leadership

Strong leadership committed to anti-corruption reforms is a common thread in these success stories.

15.5.2 Public Engagement

Public awareness, engagement, and support for anti-corruption measures are crucial for success.

15.5.3 International Cooperation

Many successful efforts benefit from international partnerships and cooperation to combat cross-border corruption.

15.6 Sustaining Progress and Future Challenges

15.6.1 Ongoing Vigilance

Sustaining progress in the fight against corruption requires ongoing vigilance, as corruption can resurface if not consistently addressed.

15.6.2 Complex Challenges

New challenges, such as cybercrime and money laundering, require innovative approaches to combat corruption effectively.

15.6.3 Global Collaboration

The success stories underscore the importance of global collaboration in the fight against corruption and the need for countries to learn from one another's experiences.

15.7 Conclusion

These success stories demonstrate that progress in the fight against corruption is possible. By implementing comprehensive reforms, fostering transparency, and engaging the public, nations and institutions can significantly reduce corruption and create a more just and accountable society.

CHAPTER TEN

Transparency and Accountability

Exploring the Vital Role of Transparency and Accountability in Preventing Corruption

Transparency and accountability are crucial pillars in the fight against corruption, as they help deter corrupt practices, expose wrongdoers, and promote good governance. In this chapter, we delve into the significance of transparency and accountability in preventing corruption and promoting a culture of integrity.

16.1 Transparency: Shedding Light on Governance

16.1.1 Definition and Principles

Transparency refers to the openness and accessibility of government actions, decisions, and information to the public. Principles include access to information, open data, and public disclosure.

16.1.2 Transparency in Public Finances

Transparent budgeting and financial reporting are essential for ensuring that public funds are used efficiently and without corruption.

16.1.3 Access to Government Information

Freedom of information laws empower citizens to access government records, promoting transparency in decision-making.

16.1.4 Whistleblower Protections

Effective whistleblower protection mechanisms encourage individuals to report corruption and misconduct without fear of retaliation.

16.2 Accountability: Holding the Powerful Responsible

16.2.1 Definition and Mechanisms

Accountability involves holding individuals and institutions responsible for their actions and decisions. Mechanisms include oversight, checks and balances, and legal accountability.

16.2.2 Independent Auditing

Independent auditing bodies play a crucial role in holding government agencies accountable for their use of public funds.

16.2.3 Parliamentary Oversight

Legislatures can exercise oversight by scrutinizing government actions, budgets, and policies to ensure they align with the public interest.

16.2.4 Judicial Accountability

An independent judiciary is essential for ensuring legal accountability, with the power to review government actions and uphold the rule of law.

16.3 Preventing Corruption Through Transparency and Accountability

16.3.1 Deterrence Effect

Transparency and accountability mechanisms create a deterrent effect, dissuading individuals and institutions from engaging in corrupt practices.

16.3.2 Early Detection

Transparency allows for the early detection of irregularities, enabling timely intervention and preventing corruption from becoming entrenched.

16.3.3 Promoting Ethical Behavior

Transparent and accountable governance sets a positive example and promotes ethical behavior within public and private sectors.

16.3.4 Citizen Engagement

Transparency and accountability mechanisms encourage citizen engagement, fostering an active and informed citizenry that can hold officials and institutions accountable.

16.4 International Transparency and Accountability Initiatives

16.4.1 Open Government Partnership (OGP)

OGP is a global initiative that promotes government transparency, citizen engagement, and accountability through national action plans.

16.4.2 Extractive Industries Transparency Initiative (EITI)

EITI encourages transparency in the extractive industries to prevent corruption related to resource extraction.

16.4.3 Global Anti-Corruption Initiatives

Organizations like Transparency International and the World Bank support global anti-corruption initiatives, advocating for transparency and accountability measures.

16.5 Challenges and Barriers

16.5.1 Resistance to Transparency

Some governments and institutions resist transparency and accountability measures due to concerns about political exposure and loss of control.

16.5.2 Capacity Constraints

Building the capacity for transparency and accountability can be challenging, particularly in countries with limited resources or capacity.

16.5.3 Cultural and Political Factors

Cultural norms and political dynamics may hinder the adoption of transparency and accountability practices in some regions.

16.6 Conclusion

Transparency and accountability are indispensable tools in preventing corruption and promoting good governance. By embracing these principles, societies can create a culture of integrity, build public trust, and ensure that public resources are used for the benefit of all citizens.

Examining the Courageous Role of Whistleblowers in Uncovering Corruption

Whistleblowers play a critical role in exposing corruption by bringing to light hidden wrongdoing within organizations, institutions, and governments. In this chapter, we explore the importance of whistleblowers, the challenges they face, and the impact they have on combating corruption.

17.1 Who Are Whistleblowers?

17.1.1 Defining Whistleblowers

Whistleblowers are individuals who report misconduct, illegal activities, or corruption within their organizations or institutions, often at great personal risk.

17.1.2 Motivations

Whistleblowers are motivated by a commitment to ethical values, a desire for justice, and a sense of responsibility to society.

17.2 The Role of Whistleblowers in Exposing Corruption

17.2.1 Early Detection

Whistleblowers often serve as the first line of defense against corruption by detecting and reporting irregularities before they become entrenched.

17.2.2 Uncovering Hidden Truths

Whistleblowers have the potential to reveal hidden corruption, exposing wrongdoers and their actions to public scrutiny.

17.2.3 Fostering Accountability

Whistleblowers hold individuals and institutions accountable for their actions, contributing to transparency and good governance.

17.2.4 Catalysts for Change

Whistleblowers can catalyze reforms within organizations and institutions, leading to increased integrity and ethical behavior.

17.3 Challenges Faced by Whistleblowers

17.3.1 Retaliation and Reprisals

Whistleblowers often face retaliation, including job loss, harassment, and threats, making their actions courageous but perilous.

17.3.2 Legal Protections

Many countries have whistleblower protection laws, but the effectiveness of these laws can vary, leaving whistleblowers vulnerable.

17.3.3 Emotional and Psychological Toll

Whistleblowing can take a significant emotional and psychological toll on individuals, affecting their mental well-being.

17.4 Whistleblower Protections and Support

17.4.1 Legal Protections

Robust whistleblower protection laws safeguard whistleblowers from retaliation and provide legal remedies for those who face reprisals.

17.4.2 Anonymity and Confidentiality

Protecting the identity and confidentiality of whistleblowers is essential to ensure their safety.

17.4.3 Support Networks

Whistleblower support organizations and networks offer assistance, legal counsel, and psychological support to individuals facing challenges.

17.4.4 Public Awareness and Advocacy

Raising public awareness about the importance of whistleblowers and advocating for their rights can strengthen protections.

17.5 Impact and Success Stories

17.5.1 High-Profile Cases

High-profile whistleblower cases have led to significant revelations and consequences, such as the exposure of financial fraud and corporate wrongdoing.

17.5.2 Legislative Reforms

Whistleblowers have been instrumental in driving legislative reforms aimed at enhancing transparency and accountability.

17.5.3 Corporate and Institutional Changes

Whistleblowers have sparked changes within organizations and institutions, leading to improved ethical standards and practices.

17.6 The Ethical Dilemma of Whistleblowing

17.6.1 Balancing Loyalty and Responsibility

Whistleblowers often grapple with the ethical dilemma of loyalty to their organizations versus their responsibility to expose wrongdoing.

17.6.2 Ethical Considerations for Organizations

Organizations must consider ethical practices and create a culture that encourages internal reporting of misconduct.

17.7 Conclusion

Whistleblowers are courageous individuals who play a vital role in the fight against corruption. By recognizing their contributions, strengthening legal protections, and fostering a culture of accountability, societies can empower whistleblowers to expose corruption and promote integrity within organizations and institutions.

Exploring Strategies to Foster Ethical Behavior and Uphold Integrity

Promoting ethical behavior and upholding integrity are essential for preventing corruption and ensuring the well-being of societies. In this chapter, we examine various strategies and initiatives that individuals, organizations, and governments can implement to foster ethics and integrity.

18.1 The Importance of Ethical Behavior

18.1.1 Defining Ethics

Ethics refer to the principles, values, and moral standards that guide human behavior and decision-making.

18.1.2 The Role of Ethics in Society

Ethics serve as the foundation for trust, fairness, and cooperation within communities and institutions.

18.1.3 The Consequences of Unethical Behavior

Unethical behavior, such as corruption, can have severe consequences, eroding trust, and damaging individuals and institutions.

18.2 Strategies for Promoting Ethical Behavior

18.2.1 Ethical Leadership

Leaders set the tone for ethical behavior within organizations and institutions, leading by example and promoting ethical values.

18.2.2 Codes of Conduct and Ethics Training

Organizations can establish codes of conduct and provide ethics training to employees, emphasizing the importance of ethical decision-making.

18.2.3 Whistleblower Protections

Robust whistleblower protections encourage employees to report unethical behavior without fear of retaliation.

18.2.4 Transparent Governance

Transparency in decision-making and governance processes reduces opportunities for corruption and fosters ethical behavior.

18.3 The Role of Education

18.3.1 Ethics Education

Integrating ethics education into school curricula and workplace training programs instills ethical values from an early age.

18.3.2 Professional Ethics

Professional organizations can develop and enforce codes of ethics for their members, promoting ethical behavior within specific industries.

18.4 Government Initiatives

18.4.1 Anti-Corruption Agencies

Governments can establish and support independent anti-corruption agencies to enforce ethical behavior and combat corruption.

18.4.2 Regulatory Frameworks

Effective regulatory frameworks, including anti-corruption laws and enforcement mechanisms, deter unethical practices.

18.4.3 Public Awareness Campaigns

Government-led public awareness campaigns can educate citizens about the importance of ethics and integrity.

18.5 Corporate Social Responsibility (CSR)

18.5.1 Ethical Business Practices

Companies can embrace CSR by adopting ethical business practices, ensuring fair treatment of employees, and reducing their environmental impact.

18.5.2 Stakeholder Engagement

Engaging with stakeholders, including employees, customers, and communities, promotes transparency and accountability.

18.6 Ethical Decision-Making

18.6.1 Ethical Frameworks

Individuals and organizations can use ethical frameworks and decision-making tools to evaluate the morality of their actions.

18.6.2 Ethical Dilemmas

Ethical dilemmas may arise in complex situations, and individuals must navigate them by considering the ethical implications of their choices.

18.7 Success Stories in Promoting Ethical Behavior

18.7.1 Ethical Leadership

Examples of ethical leaders who have steered organizations toward ethical practices and integrity.

18.7.2 Corporate Responsibility

Instances of companies that have embraced CSR and ethical business practices.

18.7.3 Government Initiatives

Government-led initiatives that have successfully promoted ethics and integrity in public service.

18.8 Challenges and Ongoing Efforts

18.8.1 Resistance to Change

Resistance to ethical reforms within organizations and institutions can be a significant challenge.

18.8.2 Cultural and Contextual Factors

Cultural norms and contextual factors may impact the adoption of ethical behaviors and practices.

18.8.3 Long-Term Commitment

Promoting ethical behavior requires a long-term commitment from individuals, organizations, and governments.

18.9 Conclusion

Promoting ethical behavior and upholding integrity are critical for building trust, preventing corruption, and fostering a just and prosperous society. By embracing ethical leadership, education, government initiatives, and corporate responsibility, societies can create a culture of ethics and integrity that benefits all members.

CHAPTER ELEVEN

Looking Ahead: Can Corruption Be Eradicated?

Assessing the Prospects of a Corruption-Free Future

The prospect of a world without corruption is an ambitious but essential goal. In this final chapter, we explore the challenges, opportunities, and strategies for achieving a corruption-free future, assessing whether complete eradication is feasible and what steps can be taken to move closer to that vision.

19.1 The Elusive Goal of Eradicating Corruption

19.1.1 Defining Eradication

What does it mean to eradicate corruption, and can it truly be achieved?

19.1.2 Historical Perspectives

Examining past efforts and milestones in the fight against corruption and their impact.

19.1.3 Persistent Challenges

Identifying the enduring challenges and obstacles to eliminating corruption at all levels of society.

19.2 The Role of Technology and Innovation

19.2.1 Transparency Technologies

How emerging technologies like blockchain and data analytics can enhance transparency and traceability.

19.2.2 Digital Governance

The potential of e-governance and digital platforms in reducing corruption through streamlined processes and increased accountability.

19.2.3 AI and Predictive Analytics

The use of artificial intelligence and predictive analytics in identifying corruption risks and patterns.

19.3 The Importance of Global Cooperation

19.3.1 International Agreements

Assessing the impact of international agreements and organizations in the fight against cross-border corruption.

19.3.2 Mutual Legal Assistance

The need for strengthened mutual legal assistance and information sharing among nations.

19.3.3 Civil Society and Grassroots Movements

The role of civil society organizations and grassroots movements in advocating for anti-corruption measures.

19.4 Balancing Enforcement and Prevention

19.4.1 Prosecution and Deterrence

The importance of strong enforcement mechanisms and the deterrence effect of legal consequences.

19.4.2 Preventive Measures

The value of preventive measures, such as ethics education and fostering a culture of integrity.

19.5 Ethical Leadership and Public Engagement

19.5.1 Leadership Accountability

The role of leaders in upholding ethical standards and being accountable for their actions.

19.5.2 Public Awareness

The significance of raising public awareness about the consequences of corruption and the benefits of integrity.

19.6 The Challenge of Cultural Change

19.6.1 Cultural Norms

Addressing the influence of cultural norms that may tolerate or even encourage corrupt practices.

19.6.2 Shifting Mindsets

Strategies for shifting societal mindsets toward a greater emphasis on ethics and integrity.

19.7 Measuring Progress and Success

19.7.1 Corruption Indices

How corruption indices and measurements help assess progress and identify areas for improvement.

19.7.2 Success Stories

Highlighting countries and regions that have made significant strides in reducing corruption.

19.8 The Way Forward

19.8.1 Realistic Expectations

Setting realistic expectations for the gradual reduction, if not complete eradication, of corruption.

19.8.2 Continuous Vigilance

Emphasizing the need for ongoing vigilance and sustained efforts in the fight against corruption.

19.8.3 Hope for a Better Future

Concluding with a hopeful perspective on the potential for a world with reduced corruption and enhanced integrity.

19.9 Conclusion

The journey toward a corruption-free world is arduous, but it is a journey worth undertaking. By embracing technological innovations, fostering global cooperation, promoting ethical leadership, and addressing cultural norms, societies can move closer to the ideal of a future where corruption is significantly reduced, if not eradicated entirely.

Examining Persistent Hurdles in the Fight Against Corruption

The battle against corruption is an ongoing struggle that faces numerous challenges. In this chapter, we delve into the persistent hurdles and complexities that hinder efforts to combat corruption effectively, and explore strategies to address these challenges.

12.1 The Resilience of Corruption

12.1.1 Corruption's Adaptability

How corruption evolves and adapts to new circumstances, making it difficult to eradicate.

12.1.2 Hidden and Covert Practices

The prevalence of covert corruption practices that are harder to detect and expose.

12.1.3 Resistance to Change

The resistance from entrenched interests that benefit from corrupt systems and are reluctant to reform.

12.2 Political Interference

12.2.1 Political Will

The importance of political will in addressing corruption and the challenges posed by politicians who resist anti-corruption efforts.

12.2.2 Politicization of Anti-Corruption Agencies

How some governments may interfere with the independence and effectiveness of anti-corruption agencies.

12.2.3 Impunity of High-Ranking Officials

The difficulty of holding high-ranking officials accountable for corrupt practices.

12.3 The Role of Money Laundering

12.3.1 Sophisticated Money Laundering Schemes

The use of increasingly sophisticated methods to launder corruptly obtained funds.

12.3.2 Cross-Border Money Laundering

The challenge of tracking and recovering illicit assets that cross international borders.

12.3.3 Collaboration with Enablers

The role of financial institutions and professionals in facilitating money laundering.

12.4 Whistleblower Protection and Support

12.4.1 Insufficient Protections

The inadequacy of whistleblower protection laws and mechanisms in some countries.

12.4.2 Fear of Retaliation

The continued fear of retaliation that deters potential whistleblowers from coming forward.

12.4.3 Psychological and Emotional Toll

The emotional and psychological toll that whistleblowing can take on individuals.

12.5 International Cooperation and Jurisdictional Challenges

12.5.1 Limited Cross-Border Cooperation

The challenges of coordinating anti-corruption efforts across different jurisdictions.

12.5.2 Safe Havens for Ill-Gotten Assets

The existence of offshore financial centers that provide safe havens for corruptly obtained assets.

12.5.3 Legal and Cultural Differences

The discrepancies in legal systems and cultural norms that affect international cooperation.

12.6 The Importance of Civil Society and Media

12.6.1 Threats to Civil Society

The threats and restrictions faced by civil society organizations and independent media in some countries.

12.6.2 Civil Society's Role in Advocacy

The vital role of civil society and media in advocating for anti-corruption measures and raising public awareness.

12.7 The Long-Term Nature of the Battle

12.7.1 Gradual Progress

Recognizing that the fight against corruption is a long-term endeavor with incremental progress.

12.7.2 Continuous Vigilance

The need for sustained vigilance and commitment to anti-corruption efforts.

12.7.3 Hope for the Future

Maintaining hope for a future with reduced corruption despite ongoing challenges.

12.8 Conclusion

The battle against corruption is fraught with ongoing challenges, but it remains a crucial endeavor for the well-being of societies worldwide.

By addressing political interference, strengthening whistleblower protections, enhancing international cooperation, and supporting civil society and media, progress can be made in the fight against corruption, even in the face of persistent hurdles.

Exploring the Collective Efforts Needed to Foster Transparency and Ethics

Creating a more transparent and ethical world requires the concerted efforts of individuals, organizations, and governments. In this chapter, we examine the roles and responsibilities of each stakeholder group and how they can collectively contribute to a world characterized by integrity and transparency.

13.1 The Power of Individual Actions

13.1.1 Ethical Decision-Making

The importance of individuals making ethical choices in their personal and professional lives.

13.1.2 Whistleblowing

The role of individuals in reporting corruption and unethical behavior when they encounter it.

13.1.3 Civic Engagement

How individuals can engage in civic activities and advocate for ethical practices in their communities.

13.2 The Responsibility of Organizations

13.2.1 Establishing Ethical Cultures

The obligation of organizations to foster ethical cultures that prioritize integrity, fairness, and transparency.

13.2.2 Codes of Conduct

The development and enforcement of codes of conduct and ethics policies within organizations.

13.2.3 Embracing Corporate Social Responsibility

The role of businesses in promoting corporate social responsibility (CSR) and sustainable practices.

13.2.4 Whistleblower Protection

Ensuring that organizations have robust whistleblower protection mechanisms in place.

13.3 The Duty of Governments

13.3.1 Enacting Strong Anti-Corruption Laws

Governments should establish and enforce anti-corruption laws and regulations that deter corrupt practices.

13.3.2 Supporting Independent Oversight

The importance of governments supporting independent oversight bodies and anti-corruption agencies.

13.3.3 Transparency and Accountability

Governments should prioritize transparency in decision-making and accountability for public officials.

13.3.4 International Cooperation

The role of governments in cooperating with international partners to combat cross-border corruption.

13.4 Collaboration Among Stakeholders

13.4.1 Public-Private Partnerships

Encouraging partnerships between governments and businesses to promote ethical behavior and transparency.

13.4.2 Civil Society Engagement

Governments and organizations should actively engage with civil society and non-governmental organizations (NGOs) to strengthen anti-corruption efforts.

13.4.3 Media and Public Awareness

The media plays a vital role in exposing corruption, and governments and organizations should support investigative journalism and public awareness campaigns.

13.5 Measuring Progress

13.5.1 Corruption Indices

How indices like the Corruption Perceptions Index can measure progress and identify areas for improvement.

13.5.2 Reporting and Transparency

The role of reporting mechanisms and transparency in tracking and communicating progress.

13.6 The Long-Term Vision

13.6.1 Commitment to Sustainability

The need for a sustained commitment to ethical and transparent practices over the long term.

13.6.2 Hope for Future Generations

The aspiration for a more transparent and ethical world as a legacy for future generations.

13.7 Conclusion

Creating a more transparent and ethical world is a collective endeavor that demands action from individuals, organizations, and governments alike. By embracing ethical decision-making, fostering ethical cultures, enacting strong anti-corruption laws, and collaborating across sectors, stakeholders can work together to build a world characterized by integrity, fairness, and transparency.

Epilogue: Towards A World Of Integrity And Transparency

In our journey through the complex and multifaceted terrain of corruption, we have explored its definitions, origins, forms, and global impact. We've examined the psychological and sociological factors that contribute to corruption and uncovered the insidious ways it infiltrates governments, corporations, and even law enforcement agencies.

We've delved into the cases of individuals and entities that have succumbed to the seduction of ill-gotten gains, and we've celebrated those who, often at great personal risk, exposed corruption's hidden truths.

Our exploration has revealed the far-reaching consequences of corruption, affecting economic development, social stability, and the very fabric of trust within societies. The human cost of corruption is not measured solely in financial terms but in the suffering, injustice, and lost opportunities it inflicts on individuals and communities.

Yet, amidst these challenges, we have also encountered stories of hope and resilience. From countries that have transformed their governance and institutions to businesses that have chosen integrity over profit, there are success stories that remind us of the potential for positive change.

The battle against corruption is far from over, and it is one that requires the ongoing dedication of individuals, organizations, and governments. Transparency, accountability, and ethical behavior are our allies in this fight, but they must be actively cultivated, enforced, and championed by all stakeholders. The role of whistleblowers in exposing corruption demonstrates the power of individuals in making a difference, and their protection is essential for the health of our institutions.

International cooperation and the shared commitment to anti-corruption efforts can help bridge the gaps in our defenses against corrupt practices. We've seen that, while challenges persist, progress is possible. A world with reduced corruption and enhanced integrity is a vision worth pursuing for the sake of present and future generations.

As we conclude our exploration, it's important to remember that the path to a more transparent and ethical world is an ongoing journey. Each one of us can contribute to this vision, whether through ethical choices in our daily lives, supporting organizations that champion transparency, or holding governments accountable for their actions. With collective effort, vigilance, and a shared commitment to integrity, we can move closer to a world where the shadows of corruption grow ever dimmer, and the light of transparency and ethics shines brighter.

The story of corruption is not yet concluded, but we hold the pen to write the next chapter. May it be a chapter of progress, hope, and the relentless pursuit of a world characterized by integrity and transparency.

······***······